Student Workbook and Study Guide to Accompany

RESEARCH DESIGN AND METHODS
A PROCESS APPROACH

Fourth Edition

Kenneth S. Bordens
Bruce B. Abbott
Indiana University—Purdue University, Fort Wayne

Mayfield Publishing Company
Mountain View, California
London • Toronto

International Standard Book Number: 0-7674-0508-0

Manufactured in the United States of America
10 9 8 7 6 5 4 3 2

Mayfield Publishing Company
1280 Villa Street
Mountain View, California 94041

CONTENTS

TO THE STUDENT

When we wrote the first three editions of *Research Design and Methods: A Process Approach,* we hoped that students would experience firsthand the fascinating and exciting world of research. Our hope has remained the same as we have prepared the fourth edition. To help you master the concepts in the textbook, we have prepared this accompanying study guide.

Beginning each chapter of this study guide is a section called "Key Questions to Consider." In this section, we have identified the central questions that you should consider when reading the text, those that are most important to your understanding of the research process. After the list of questions, you will find a chapter outline of the corresponding chapter in the text. This outline can help you organize your reading and study time.

After the chapter outline are "Review and Study Questions," which will help you prepare for exams. There are four types of questions, outlined as follows.

Key Term Definition

We have listed the key terms from each chapter for you to define. After reading the text, try to define each term without looking at the text definition. It is best if you define each term *in your own words* by paraphrasing the text's definition. Try to supply an example for each term. Actively transforming the information in the text into your own thoughts and ideas will help you understand the terms better than simply memorizing and writing down the text definition. After you have defined each term, use the text chapter and the glossary at the end of the text to check your work.

Multiple-Choice Questions

In your college career you will probably encounter many multiple-choice exams, especially in larger classes. Your instructor in your research methods course may use such items, even if your class is small. The multiple-choice questions we have included in this study guide will help you in two ways. First and foremost, they will help you learn the material in the text. Second, they will give you practice doing multiple-choice tests. A few basic rules will help you master these items.

First, be sure to read each question completely and carefully. That includes the stem of the question as well as each choice. We have in our years of teaching run into many students who get multiple-choice items incorrect because they do not carefully read the question. Read the stem of the question looking very specifically for what is being asked.

1. Is the question being asked in the affirmative (for example, "Which of the following is an example of . . . ?") or in the negative (for example, "Which of the following is not an example of . . .")?

2. Consider *all* the possibilities, noting carefully how the alternatives are worded. Don't be fooled by "alternative a" that sounds correct and then neglect to read the rest of the alternatives. There may be a better alternative among b, c, and d (or perhaps the correct answer is "both a and b").

3. Don't read too much into the question. Often students think their instructors are trying to trick them by including items that could be answered in several ways if certain, unlikely conditions exist. As a general rule, accept the most likely meaning. If you are really unsure what is being asked of you, ask your instructor about the item in question.

Second, after reading each alternative, eliminate those that are obviously incorrect. If you can eliminate one or two choices as obviously incorrect, you need consider only the remaining ones seriously.

Third, trust your intuition. If you do not know the answer to a question and take a "stab" at the answer, don't go back later and change your answer unless you have good reason to do so. For example, you may encounter an item later on an exam that triggers your memory for the previous item. If you have good reason to change an answer, do so, but do not try to second-guess yourself. Most of the time your first guess is probably correct.

At the end of each chapter in this study guide we have listed the correct answers to the multiple-choice items. Of course you should not look at them until you have done all of the items. Evaluate your answers against the correct answers. Try to understand why you got certain ones wrong. Use the text to help explain the correct answer. Of course, you should always feel free to ask your instructor for clarification of any points you do not understand.

Fill-in Questions

Multiple-choice items require you to recognize a correct answer. We also include items that require you to recall an answer. Fill-in questions do this better than multiple-choice questions. For each item, provide the word or phrase that best completes the sentence. After doing all the items, check your answers against the correct answers listed at the end of the chapter.

Essay Questions

Term definitions, multiple-choice questions, and fill-in items are good ways to test how well you remember information. They do not, however, help you to integrate information. Essay items do this much better. Because your instructor may require you to do essay items on a exam, we have included five or six essay questions for each chapter. When answering these questions, try to organize your answer carefully. You can know all about a topic, yet still receive a low grade because you did not organize your answer. Take the time to prepare a brief outline (even if only in your mind) for your answer before writing anything down. Then begin to answer the question. Keep in mind that you should focus on the issue central to the question. An essay item is not an invitation to regurgitate everything you can remember. Just answer the question!

Exercising Your Knowledge

Review and study questions are fine ways to help learn about the research process. However, we want you to get some "hands-on" experience with the issues raised in each chapter. The best way to learn about research is to get involved with it. Only then will you see the exciting aspects of the research process. To this end, we have included one or more exercises for each chapter that you can *do on your own*. These exercises do not require that you work in a group (although you could certainly adapt them for a group project). They are things that you can do alone to apply what you have learned and thus gain a deeper understanding of the issues in each chapter.

As you go through the exercises, you will find that some are relatively simple (for example, identifying the appropriate statistic for a given design), whereas others are more involved (for example, conducting a correlational study of the relationship between weather and mood). We urge you to do some, if not all, of these exercises, even though they consume some time. In the end you will have a much better understanding of research issues if you do the exercises than if you do not.

CHAPTER 1
EXPLAINING BEHAVIOR

KEY QUESTIONS TO CONSIDER

- What are the two steps suggested by Cialdini (1994) for exploring the causes of behavior and how do they relate to explaining behavior?
- What are the main characteristics of a scientific explanation?
- How do scientific and commonsense explanations differ?
- How do belief-based and scientific explanations differ?
- What kinds of questions do scientists refrain from investigating?
- How can faulty inference invalidate a scientific explanation?
- What are pseudoexplanations and how do you avoid them?
- What are the defining characteristics and weaknesses of the method of authority and rational method?
- What is the scientific method and why is it preferred in science?
- What is the difference between a method and a technique?
- How do basic and applied research differ? How are they similar?
- How are the steps of the scientific method applied to answering research questions?

CHAPTER OUTLINE

Exploring the Causes of Behavior
Explaining Behavior
    Scientific Explanations
        Scientific Explanations Are Empirical
        Scientific Explanations Are Rational
        Scientific Explanations Are Testable
        Scientific Explanations Are Parsimonious
        Scientific Explanations Are General
        Scientific Explanations Are Tentative

REVIEW AND STUDY QUESTIONS

Key Term Definition

Define each of the following terms.

Research:

Scientific explanation:

Parsimonious explanation:

Commonsense explanation:

Belief-based explanation:

Pseudoexplanation:

Circular explanation:

Method of authority:

Rational method:

Scientific method:

Variable:

Hypothesis:

Basic research:

Applied research:

Deductive reasoning:

Pilot study:

MULTIPLE-CHOICE QUESTIONS

Circle the alternative that best completes the stem of each question.

1. Scientific explanations are based on objective and systematic observations carried out under carefully controlled conditions. This quality makes scientific explanations
   a. rational.
   b. parsimonious.
   c. empirical.
   d. general.

2. A scientific explanation that is _____ is the least complex, requiring the fewest assumptions.
   a. empirical
   b. parsimonious
   c. general
   d. testable

3. Explanations that are simple and based on the limited information available from a situation observed are
   a. pseudoexplanations.
   b. circular explanations.
   c. commonsense explanations.
   d. authoritative explanations.

4. Scientific explanations differ from nonscientific explanations in that scientific explanations are
   a. less general.
   b. subjected to rigorous research scrutiny.
   c. more likely to be based on hearsay and anecdotal evidence.
   d. both a and b above

5. The "urban apathy" explanation for Kitty Genovese's murder shows that
   a. even scientific explanations sometimes fail.
   b. commonsense explanations do not provide an adequate explanation for observed behavior.
   c. it is difficult to avoid the trap of pseudoexplanations.
   d. none of the above

6. Explanations based on belief
   a. need no evidence to support them.
   b. are often trusted because they seem to fit with the larger framework of belief.
   c. can never be tested empirically.
   d. both a and b
   e. both b and c

7. Scientific explanations sometimes fail because they
   a. sometimes are based on inferring underlying causes from observed events.
   b. are too general.
   c. are too heavily rooted in a flawed belief system.
   d. are difficult to develop into testable hypotheses.

8. When an explanatory concept is nothing more than a new label for an existing phenomenon, we have a(n)
   a. pseudoexplanation.
   b. inferred explanation.
   c. commonsense explanation.
   d. alternative explanation.

9. To avoid the trap of circular explanations, you should
   a. include more than one independent variable in your experiment.
   b. avoid using correlational research designs.
   c. provide independent measures of the behavior of interest and the explanatory concept.
   d. place a higher premium on maintaining internal validity than external validity.

10. After reading about a terrorist attack against a passenger airliner, you go to the library and read about the factors contributing to such behavior. The method of inquiry you are using is the
    a. rational method.
    b. scientific method.
    c. exploratory method.
    d. method of authority.

11. The "rational method" of inquiry is most useful in the early stages of science to
    a. identify potential causal relationships among variables.
    b. develop hypotheses that will be subjected to empirical test.
    c. help you decide which research questions are important and which are not.
    d. none of the above

12. The scientific method of inquiry differs from other methods of inquiry in that the scientific method
    a. requires that hypotheses be tested empirically.
    b. is limited to experimental research.
    c. does not require revision and retesting of hypotheses that are not fully supported.
    d. all of the above

13. Any characteristic or quantity that can take on several different values is a
    a. variable.
    b. constant.
    c. hypothetical value.
    d. none of the above

14. A hypothesis is
    a. a statement of the actual relationship between variables.
    b. a tentative statement about the relationship between variables.
    c. tested only if it is not supported using the method of authority or rational method.
    d. none of the above

15. The point where the scientific method differs from the other methods of inquiry is
    a. initial observation of a phenomenon under real-world conditions.
    b. formulation of tentative explanations for observed phenomena.
    c. further observing and experimenting on an observed phenomenon.
    d. refining and retesting tentative explanations.

16. Imagine that you have conducted an experiment and confirmed your hypothesis. If you were using the scientific method, your next step would probably be to
    a. abandon your line of research and start a whole new research program.
    b. refine your hypothesis and further study the behavior of interest.
    c. do your experiment again because your results were probably in error.
    d. none of the above

17. Research that is conducted to test a purely theoretical issue is termed
    a. applied research.
    b. laboratory research.
    c. basic research.
    d. fundamental research.

18. Dr. Jones conducts an experiment to help a local corporation solve some production problems. This experiment would best be classified as
    a. basic research.
    b. fundamental research.
    c. pilot research.
    d. applied research.

19. The first step in the research process is
    a. choosing a research design.
    b. deciding on which statistics you want to use to analyze your data.
    c. lining up participants for your study.
    d. developing a research idea and hypothesis.

20. Hypothesis development involves deductive reasoning, which is deriving
    a. general laws from specific instances.
    b. general hypotheses from specific theories.
    c. specific hypotheses from specific ideas.
    d. specific hypotheses from general ideas.

Fill-In Questions

Fill in the blanks with the word or phrase that best completes each sentence.

1. A danger of relying on explanations based on everyday observations is that they may

   _____.

2. A(n) _____ is constantly evaluated for consistency with existing evidence and with known principles.

3. Although we develop explanations for behavior every day, these explanations do not qualify as truly _____.

4. Scientists prefer explanations that have broad explanatory power over those that work only within a limited set of circumstances. This suggests that scientific explanations are

    _____.

5. A(n) _____ requires no evidence and is assumed to be true.

6. The mythical scientist in the *Motel of the Mysteries* example used in the text developed faulty explanations because he relied on _____ too much.

7. Faulty conclusions may be drawn from research data because researchers fail to consider

    _____.

8. Using the label "schizophrenia" to "explain" why a person is hallucinating and acting in a bizarre manner is an example of using a(n) _____.

9. Pseudoexplanations can be avoided by providing _____ of the behavior of interest and the explanatory concept.

10. In the _____, you rely on expert sources for answers to questions.

11. The _____ method is the only acceptable method of developing valid scientific explanations.

12. When using the scientific method, the hypothesis that you develop is subjected to

    _____.

13. An alternative to discarding a disconfirmed hypothesis is to _____

    _____.

14. In addition to being a method of inquiry, the scientific method is also a(n) _____

    _____.

15. Even though we can sometimes classify research as basic or applied, the distinction between these two categories is often _____.

Essay Questions

1. Why is a scientific explanation stronger than a commonsense explanation?

2. Give an example of a pseudoexplanation (other than one provided in the text), and show how the trap of pseudoexplanation can be avoided.

3. What are the critical differences between the nonscientific (for example, the method of authority) methods and the scientific method?

4. Outline and discuss the steps of the scientific method, and indicate why each is so important.

5. Compare and contrast basic and applied research.

6. What steps would you follow if you wanted to design an experiment on a topic that interests you? What are some of the major decisions you would have to make?

EXERCISING YOUR KNOWLEDGE

Developing and Testing Hypotheses

One characteristic of the scientific method is to develop a testable hypothesis. Research is then used to test the validity of that hypothesis. This exercise will give you practice in developing and testing hypotheses. It is based on experiments on concept formation reported by Bruner, Goodnow, and Austin (1956). In a typical concept formation task, a participant is shown an example from a category (for example, a geometric form), and from an array of stimuli the participant must then discover the characteristics of objects constituting a category.

Figure 1-1 shows an array of stimuli used by Bruner et al. in their studies of thought processes. Represented are four dimensions with three variations of each. These are shape of object (circle, square, or cross), color of object (black, white, shaded), number of objects (one, two, or three), and the number of borders surrounding the objects (one, two, or three). Each item ("card") in the array represents an instance of some category. Your task, as outlined next, will be to discover the general rule of class membership.

For this exercise we have thought of three categories. Of course, we are not going to tell you what they are at this point. We will tell you that the following instances in Figure 1-1 are examples of these three categories (referred to by "row, column"; for example, "1, 3" refers to the instance at the intersection of row 1 and column 3 in Figure 1-1):

1. 4, 4
2. 5, 6
3. 5, 9

Take each of these categories one at a time and do the following:

1. Develop a hypothesis about the characteristics of the general category and record your hypothesis.

2. Choose an instance from the array that you think adequately tests your hypothesis.

3. Consult Table 1, 2, or 3 at the back of this manual (depending on which category you are trying to discover) for feedback as to whether your choice is also a member of the category. Do this by looking up your choice in the appropriate row and column of the correct table. For example, if you selected 7, 8 for the first category, then look up row 7, column 8 in Table 1 in

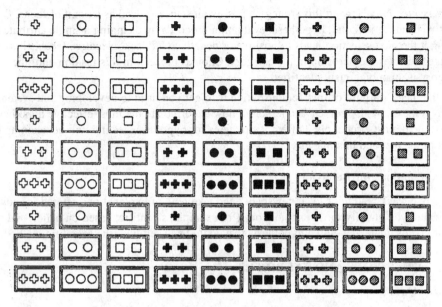

Figure 1-1 Stimuli for hypothesis-testing exercise. Reprinted from Bruner, J., Goodnow, J. J., & Austin, G. A. (1956), *A Study of Thinking* (p. 42). Copyright © 1956 by John Wiley and Sons, New York.

Appendix A. Repeat the process. *IMPORTANT: LOOK ONLY AT THE ROW AND COLUMN RELEVANT TO YOUR PRESENT CHOICE.*

4. Keep a running record of your hypotheses, how they were tested, whether or not your hypotheses are confirmed, and how many choices were required to discover the category. Try to discover the category in the fewest choices possible (the categories themselves are identified on the last page of the Appendix; now, no cheating!).

After you have completed all three of the category problems, you can then evaluate the strategy that you used to discover the category. Bruner, Goodnow, and Austin (1956) define several possible concept formation strategies:

1. *Simultaneous Scanning:* This is the most sophisticated way of testing your hypotheses. With this method the individual uses the information about the first positive card to logically eliminate as many possible rules as possible. Thereafter, choices are used to simultaneously test several hypotheses. Using this strategy leads to the fastest identification of a category. However, it is difficult to use because so much information must be considered at once.

2. *Successive Scanning:* This is the least sophisticated method. With this method one hypothesis is tested at a time. For example, you may have said "all members of the category are black" and tested that hypothesis. After disconfirming that hypothesis you may have moved on to another hypothesis (for example, "all members are circles").

3. *Conservative Focusing:* In this strategy a positive instance is used as a point of focus. Once a positive instance is found, hypothesis evaluation proceeds by changing a single attribute and seeing if the next selection leads to positive or negative feedback. Negative feedback to the change indicates membership in the category. Choices proceed in this fashion until the category is unambiguously identified.

Whereas the major purpose of this demonstration is to get you used to developing and systematically testing hypotheses, it also serves as a lesson in how to formulate the most effective hypotheses and how to test them most effectively. Different strategies for hypothesis testing will be taken up in other chapters of the text and this manual.

Identifying Explanations for Behavior

For a period of one week read your local newspaper and take note of explanations offered for covered events. How would you classify those explanations (for example, scientific, based on belief, and so on)? For each event you evaluate, develop a hypothesis that could be tested with the scientific method.

ANSWERS TO QUESTIONS AND EXERCISES

Multiple-Choice Questions

1. C	6. D	11. B	16. B
2. B	7. A	12. A	17. C
3. C	8. A	13. A	18. D
4. B	9. C	14. B	19. D
5. B	10. D	15. C	20. D

Fill-In Questions

1. become the basis for future actions
2. scientific explanation
3. scientific
4. general
5. belief-based explanation
6. inference
7. alternative explanations
8. pseudoexplanation or circular explanation
9. independent measures
10. method of authority
11. scientific
12. further observing and experimenting
13. revise and retest the hypothesis
14. attitude
15. unclear

CHAPTER 2

DEVELOPING IDEAS FOR RESEARCH

KEY QUESTIONS TO CONSIDER

- How do you use unsystematic and systematic observation to help develop research ideas?
- What makes a research question answerable and important?
- How can a thorough review of the literature help you develop good research questions?
- What is the difference between a primary and secondary source and how should each be used?
- What are the differences between nonrefereed and refereed journal articles?
- How do the major sources of research information differ?
- What are *PsycLit* and the *Psychological Abstracts* used for?
- How can you narrow or broaden a computerized literature search?
- What are the advantages and disadvantages of computer literature searches?
- Why is it important to read a research report critically?
- What rules should you follow when reading a research report critically?
- What should you look for in each section of an APA-style research report?

CHAPTER OUTLINE

Sources of Research Ideas
    Unsystematic Observation
    Systematic Observation
    Theory
    The Need to Solve Practical Problems
Developing Good Research Questions
    Asking Answerable Questions
    Asking the Right Questions
    Asking Important Questions
Reviewing the Literature
Sources of Research Information

REVIEW AND STUDY QUESTIONS

Key Term Definition

Define each of the following terms.

Theory:

Empirical question:

Operational definition:

Literature review:

Primary source:

Secondary source:

Refereed journal:

Nonrefereed journal:

Paper sessions:

Personal communications:

Psychological Abstracts:

PsycLit:

Thesaurus of Psychological Index Terms:

Multiple-Choice Questions

Circle the alternative that best completes the stem of each question.

1. Casual observation of your pet hamster's behavior would constitute what kind of observation?
   a. systematic
   b. unsystematic
   c. irrelevant
   d. experimental

2. A valuable source of *systematic* observation is
   a. informal observations of family members.
   b. your personal experiences.
   c. published research reports.
   d. the anecdotes of a friend.

3. Research ideas arise from
   a. the need to solve practical problems.
   b. theory.
   c. previous research.
   d. all of the above

4. Which of the following questions could (at least in theory) be answered using the scientific method?
   a. How many angels can stand on the head of a pin?
   b. Is abortion moral or immoral?
   c. What conditions promote agreement in a bargaining situation?
   d. Should prayer be encouraged in the public schools?

5. Which of the following would *not* qualify as an operational definition of anxiety?
   a. A score on a test designed to measure anxiety level
   b. A vague feeling of impending disaster
   c. Sympathetic nervous system activity, as indexed by perspiration, heart rate, and blood presure
   d. All of the above would qualify.

6. As a stimulus for further research, a question is probably important if
   a. it has already been satisfactorily answered by previous research.
   b. its answer can support virtually any hypothesis.
   c. answering it will clarify relationships among variables known to affect the behavioral sytem under study.
   d. there is no a priori reason to believe the variables in question are causally related.

7. Conducting a literature review before you design a research study can
   a. help you to avoid "reinventing the wheel."
   b. identify measures and apparatus you might want to use for your study.
   c. show whether your original question has already been answered.
   d. all of the above

8. A danger in relying on secondary sources for research information is that
   a. the information provided may not be up-to-date.
   b. the author of the secondary source may have misrepresented the described research.
   c. secondary sources tend not to provide enough detail about the studies they describe.
   d. all of the above

9. Which of the sources listed would provide the most *recent* information on a research topic?
   a. textbooks
   b. journal articles
   c. papers delivered at professional meetings
   d. reviews

10. Where would you obtain the most *detailed* description of the method and results of a research project?
    a. A research report in the *Journal of Experimental Psychology*
    b. A paper delivered at the annual meeting of the Midwestern Psychological Association
    c. A review article in the *Psychological Bulletin*
    d. A theoretical article in *Psychological Review*

11. An advantage of attending a paper session at a convention rather than reading about the research in a journal is that
    a. you get a more detailed description of the method.
    b. you can meet the researchers.
    c. the research has been reviewed by experts and approved.
    d. all of the above

12. If you want to look up a topic using *PsycLit* but do not know what keyword to use, you can find out by consulting
    a. the *Thesaurus of Psychological Index Terms*.
    b. *Roget's Thesaurus*.
    c. the table of contents of *Psychological Abstracts*.
    d. *Webster's Dictionary*.

13. According to your text, a drawback to using *PsycLit* is that
    a. it has only a very limited database of articles indexed.
    b. searches usually turn up very few articles.
    c. if you are not careful choosing your keywords you may turn up hundreds of citations, many of them irrelevant to your needs.
    d. all of the above

14. You would use the _____ of the *Psychological Abstracts* to look up articles on a given topic.
    a. Subject Index
    b. Source Index
    c. Topic Index
    d. Citation Index

15. The _____ of the *Social Science Citations Index* is useful for finding sources when you have very little information concerning an article.
    a. Source Index
    b. Permuterm Subject Index
    c. Citation Index
    d. Subject Index

16. According to Mayo and Lafrance (1977), when reading a research article critically you should
    a. not be overwhelmed by "cute" procedures.
    b. determine whether the results are durable.
    c. be more impressed by research that has been funded by a prestigious funding agency than by research that has not.
    d. all of the above
    e. both a and b only

17. When critically reading the method section of a research report, the "litmus test" of the method section is
    a. whether you could replicate the study from the description given.
    b. whether the method described is a standard one.
    c. the test given to the participants to determine whether they should be included in the study.
    d. any test that is administered as a part of the procedure.

Fill-In Questions

Fill in the blanks with the word or phrase that best completes each sentence.

1. Designed to account for known relationships among given variables and behavior, _____ generate new research questions through deductive reasoning.

2. Published research offers a nearly limitless source of _____ observation.

3. Your own ongoing or previous research can be a source of _____ ideas.

4. To be answerable by application of the scientific method, a question must be _____.

5. Without the use of _____ definitions, a question cannot be answered meaningfully within the scientific method.

6. A question is probably _____ if the answer can support only one among several competing hypotheses or theoretical views.

7. Before you design your study, you should always conduct a _____ _____.

8. A textbook is an example of a(n) _____ source of research information.

9. The value of secondary sources of research information (such as review articles) lies in their ability to _____, _____, and _____ results from related research studies.

10. _____ is used to do a computer search of the *Psychological Abstracts.*

11. A journal is said to be _____ if the articles it contains have been subjected to review by other researchers in the field.

12. Projects completed under contract or funded by granting agencies frequently provide a _____ of the research.

13. Personal replies by researchers to inquiries about their research come under the heading of _____.

14. The author should clearly state the purpose of a study and any hypotheses in the _____ of an APA-style paper.

15. The results of statistical hypothesis testing are presented in the _____ section of a research paper.

Essay Questions

1. Name four sources of research ideas. Describe how each source provides ideas.

2. What is the purpose of creating operational definitions for variables? If two researchers operationally defined "stress" differently, would they be measuring the same variable?

3. List three characteristics that contribute to making a research question important and three that contribute to making a research question unimportant.

4. Describe the basic strategy for carrying out a literature search.

5. Describe how you would conduct a literature review using *PsycLit.* How would you select your keywords and narrow or broaden your search?

6. Identify the parts of a research report and describe what you would find in each part.

7. When critically reading a research report, what things should you look out for in each section?

EXERCISING YOUR KNOWLEDGE

Developing a Testable Research Question

Using one of the sources of research ideas described in Chapter 2, identify a question about human or animal behavior that you might want to research. Discard any questions that cannot be addressed through observation. Next, refine the question by stating it in terms of the variables that will be

Memory for Punch Lines of Jokes

Remembering the punch line of a joke is a problem for some people, especially the elderly. Previous research indicates that punch lines are remembered better if the joke is funny than if the joke is merely stupid (Leno and Letterman, 1995). The present study examined whether the punch lines to "shaggy dog" jokes are remembered better than the punch lines to "two-liners."

Method

Participants

Twenty participants were individually tested in 1-hour sessions. Two had to be dropped from the study.

Apparatus

Participants were tested in a small, sound-isolated booth and heard the jokes presented over a loudspeaker mounted in the ceiling of the booth. The jokes were recorded on cassette tape and played back to the participants on a Sony cassette tape recorder.

Procedure

Each participant heard twenty jokes, half of the "shaggy dog" type and half of the "two liner" type. Twenty minutes after hearing the last joke, each participant was tested for memory of the punch lines.

Results

Table 1 shows the mean percentage of punch lines correctly recalled (PPLCR) and standard deviations (SD) for the two groups tested. The difference in PPLCR was statistically significant.

Table 1
Number of Punch Lines Correctly Recalled

	Shaggy Dog	Two-Liner
Mean NPLCR	6.2	8.6
SD	0.7	0.8

Participants in the "Two-Liner" group remembered the punch lines better than those in the "Shaggy Dog" group.

Discussion

The present results support the hypothesis that two-liner punch lines would be easier to remember than shaggy dog punch lines because of their quicker delivery. The results also show that elderly participants remembered the punch lines better than did younger participants, in agreement with previous data.

observed (for example, "Is depression related to the phase of the moon?"). Finally, develop an operational definition for each variable.

Reading the Literature Critically

The short paper excerpted as follows contains several major flaws. Following the suggestions given in Chapter 2 for critically reading research reports, try to identify the flaws.

Doing a Literature Search Using *PsycLit*

I. For the three following authors, find the article that matches using *PsycLit*. Try to find the articles using keywords rather than the authors' names. Write down the citation for the article including the names of the authors (last name and the initials for the first and middle names), the year of publication, the full title of the article, the name of the journal, the volume number of the journal, and the page numbers. Write out the full reference using the APA reference format.

   1. Kassin, S. M., & Dunn, M. A. (1997): Use of computer animated displays in court.
   2. Jones, S. S. (1997): Infant imitation.
   3. Peirce, K. (1997): Content of women's magazine fiction.
   4. Bailey, J. M., Kim, P. Y., Hills, A., & Linsenmeier, J. A. W. (1997): Partner preferences of gay men and lesbians.
   5. Salthouse, T. A., Hambrick, D. Z., Lukas, K. E., & Dell, T. C. (1996): Age differences on work performance.

II. Choose one of the three research areas to which these articles are relevant and find five additional reference citations using *PsycLit*. The additional references that you find must not be included in the references list attached to the article that you found in your *PsycLit* search. For each article that you find, list the following information:

   1. The keywords or names used in your search.
   2. The abstract number of each reference that you found.
   3. The full reference (using the new APA reference format) for each article that you found (author name(s), title of the article, journal name, volume, and page numbers).

III. Choose one of the five articles that you found and read it. Next, evaluate the article according to the guidelines outlined in the text.

IV. Choose any topic area that interests you and begin to generate a reference list of at least five related articles. For each article, list the information asked for in item II.

Using CARL on the Internet

Do the same exercise steps I through IV, only this time go online and use the CARL database search service <www.carl.org>. If you use both *PsycLit* and CARL note what differences there are between the two systems and which is more useful for doing literature searches.

Searching for a Book Online

You can use the Internet to search for books in university libraries. One way to do this is to follow these steps:

1. Using Yahoo, search for: University libraries.
2. Click on: Reference **Libraries:** Academic **Libraries**.
3. Scroll down the list of libraries and choose one (for example, Indiana University Bloomington).
4. Follow the instructions on how to enter and use the online catalog.
5. Search for a book using a keyword (for example, memory, eyewitness testimony).

ANSWERS TO QUESTIONS AND EXERCISES

Multiple-Choice Questions

1. B	6. C	11. B	16. E
2. C	7. D	12. A	17. A
3. D	8. D	13. C	
4. C	9. C	14. A	
5. B	10. A	15. A	

Fill-In Questions

1. theories
2. systematic
3. research
4. empirical
5. operational
6. important
7. literature review
8. secondary
9. summarize, present, and integrate
10. *PsycLit*
11. refereed
12. technical report
13. personal communication
14. introduction
15. results

Exercising Your Knowledge

Reading the Literature Critically

Introduction. No reference is given to support the assertion that elderly participants are more prone than others to forget punch lines. No rationale is given for examining the effect of joke type on memory. No hypotheses are developed or presented.

Method. The population from which participants were drawn is not given, nor the method for selecting participants to be included in the study. Why two participants were dropped is not explained. There is no description of the actual jokes used, the rate at which they were presented, volume, and so forth. No evidence is presented that the punch lines (without accompanying set up) were equally memorable. Neither memory nor the two types of jokes are operationally defined. How memory was assessed is not described.

Results. The text describes the dependent variable as "percentage of punch lines correctly recalled," yet Table 1 shows the *number* of punch lines correctly recalled. Although it is claimed that the difference between the groups was statistically significant, the statistic used to draw this conclusion is not mentioned. Neither is the level of significance reached.

Discussion. The hypothesis mentioned here was not discussed in the introduction. The results may be consistent with this hypothesis, but they do not show that the "quicker delivery" of the two-liners had anything to do with the outcome. The shaggy dog jokes were probably much longer than the two-liners, increasing the load on memory, and this increased load may be responsible for the observed outcome. The data presented were not broken down according to age of participant, so no conclusions about the effect of age on memory for punch lines can be drawn. The statement that the results concerning the effect of age agree with previous data is not supported by a reference and contradicts the information given in the introduction.

Using PsycLit or CARL

Bailey, J. M., Kim, P. Y., Hills, A., & Linsenmeier, J. A. W. (1997). Butch, femme, or straight acting? Partner preferences of gay men and lesbians. *Journal of Personality and Social Psychology, 73,* 960–973.

Jones, S. S. (1997). Imitation or exploration? Young infants' matching of adults' oral gestures. *Child Development, 67,* 1952–1969.

Kassin, S. M., & Dunn, M. A. (1997). Computer animated displays and the jury: Facilitative and prejudicial effects. *Law and Human Behavior, 21,* 269–281.

Peirce, K. (1997). Woman's magazine fiction: A content analysis of the roles, attributes, and occupations of main characters. *Sex Roles, 37,* 581–593.

Titov, N. , & Knight, R. G. (1997). Adult age differences in controlled and automatic memory processing. *Psychology and Aging, 12,* 565–573.

CHAPTER 3

CHOOSING A RESEARCH DESIGN

KEY QUESTIONS TO CONSIDER

- How are correlational and causal relationships similar and how are they different?
- What features of research allow you to draw causal inferences from your data?
- What are the defining features of correlational research?
- Why is it inappropriate to draw causal inferences from correlational data?
- Under what conditions is correlational research preferred to experimental research?
- What are the characteristics of correlational research?
- What is the relationship between the independent and dependent variables in an experiment?
- How do extraneous variables affect your research and what can you do to control them?
- What is the value of a demonstration and how does a demonstration differ from a true experiment?
- What is internal validity and why is it important?
- How do confounding variables threaten the internal validity of your research and how can they be avoided?
- What is external validity? Must all studies have strong external validity? Why or why not?
- What is a simulation and why would you use one?
- How does the realism of a simulation relate to the validity of the results obtained?
- What are the defining features of laboratory and field research?
- What are the relative advantages and disadvantages of doing laboratory and field research?

CHAPTER OUTLINE

Functions of a Research Design
Causal Versus Correlational Relationships
Correlational Research
    Characteristics of Correlational Research
    An Example of Correlational Research
        Assessing the Belsky and Rovine Study

REVIEW AND STUDY QUESTIONS

Key Term Definition

Define each of the following terms.

  Causal relationship:

Correlational relationship:

Correlational research:

Third-variable problem:

Directionality problem:

Experimental research:

Independent variable:

Treatment:

Dependent variable:

Experimental group:

Control group:

Extraneous variable:

Demonstration:

Internal validity:

Confounding:

External validity:

Simulation:

Multiple-Choice Questions

Circle the alternative that best completes the stem of each question.

1. In a _____ relationship, changes in one variable produce changes in another.
   a. causal
   b. correlational
   c. confounded
   d. unidirectional

2. Higher scores on the Scholastic Achievement Test are related to higher grades in college. This is an example of a
   a. causal relationship.
   b. correlational relationship.
   c. confounded relationship.
   d. valid relationship.

3. When two variables covary,
   a. they are causally related.
   b. one variable confounds the effects of the other.
   c. there is a weak causal relationship between them.
   d. the values of those variables change together, systematically, but may not be causally related.

4. In correlational research your main interest is to
   a. isolate and describe causal relationships among variables.
   b. control extraneous variables.
   c. demonstrate the power of an independent variable.
   d. determine whether two variables covary.

5. In correlational research
   a. independent variables are manipulated.
   b. confounding variables are included intentionally.
   c. no independent variables are manipulated.
   d. both b and c

6. Because of _____ it is dangerous to infer causality from correlational research.
   a. covariance
   b. the third-variable problem
   c. the directionality problem
   d. both b and c

7. Dr. Jones wants to study the relationship between parental attitudes about sex and teen sexual behavior. Most likely he would choose to do correlational research because
   a. it would not be possible to manipulate parental attitudes toward sex.
   b. the study could not be done in the laboratory.
   c. it would be unethical to measure sexual attitudes and behavior in an experiment.
   d. he could include more than one variable if he chose to do so.

8. The two defining characteristics of experimental research are
   a. measuring predictor and criterion variables.
   b. random assignment of participants and measuring dependent variables.
   c. manipulation of independent variables and control over extraneous variables.
   d. random assignment of participants and control over extraneous variables.

9. In an experiment on the effects of noise on problem solving, you have some participants solve a problem while being exposed to noise, whereas other participants do the same problems while not being exposed to noise. In this example, exposing or not exposing participants to the noise constitutes a(n)
   a. independent variable.
   b. dependent variable.
   c. extraneous variable.
   d. correlational variable.

10. In an experiment, the group receiving your experimental treatment is the _____ group, whereas the group not receiving the experimental treatment is the _____ group.
    a. control; experimental
    b. target; control
    c. extraneous; control
    d. experimental; control

11. In an experiment on visual perception, you make sure that your laboratory is the same temperature and has the same level of lighting throughout the experiment. This is an example of
    a. holding extraneous variables constant.
    b. manipulating an independent variable.
    c. randomly assigning participants to conditions.
    d. ignoring extraneous variables.

12. According to the text, which of the following is the greatest strength of the experimental approach?
    a. The ability to study relationships under naturally occurring conditions
    b. The ability to identify and describe causal relationships
    c. The ability to generalize results beyond the original research situation
    d. all of the above

13. A disadvantage of the experimental approach is that
    a. you cannot adequately control extraneous variables.
    b. causal relationships among variables cannot be established.
    c. your results may have limited generality.
    d. all of the above

14. If your experimental design measures what it is intended to measure, we say that the design has a high level of
    a. reliability.
    b. internal validity.
    c. ecological validity.
    d. external validity.

15. Alternative explanations for the findings of a study that may become viable because of flaws in the design are termed
    a. rival hypotheses.
    b. experimental hypotheses.
    c. theoretical possibilities.
    d. goofs.

16. When two variables combine within a study in such a way that their effects cannot be separated, the variables are said to be
    a. uncontrolled.
    b. extraneous.
    c. confounded.
    d. confused.

17. If the results of a study cannot be immediately generalized to a real-world situation or to a larger population,
    a. the study is worthless.
    b. the results tell you little of importance.
    c. they may still be of value if they indicate what can happen under given conditions or provide a test of theoretical predictions.
    d. none of the above

18. When you conduct your experiment in a laboratory (as opposed to the field) you gain _____; but you may lose some _____.
    a. reliability; validity
    b. external validity; internal validity
    c. internal validity; reliability
    d. internal validity; external validity

19. An experimental strategy that involves attempting to re-create a real-world phenomenon in the laboratory is
    a. role playing.
    b. model research.
    c. simulation.
    d. pseudoresearch.

20. Dr. Smith conducts an experiment on jury decision making. She decorates her lab so that it looks just like a real courtroom. This shows that Dr. Smith is concerned with
    a. experimental realism.
    b. actual realism.
    c. mundane realism.
    d. none of the above

21. If you were to conduct an experiment on reactions to invasions of personal space by going to the library and sitting at various distances from your participants, you would be doing a(n)
    a. field experiment.
    b. simulation experiment.
    c. observational experiment.
    d. none of the above

Fill-In Questions

Fill in the blanks with the word or phrase that best completes each sentence.

1. Your ability to distinguish between causal and correlational relationships depends on
   _____.

2. The behavior you record in a study is the _____.

3. Two ways to control the effects of extraneous variables are _____
   and _____.

4. You place the names of your participants on slips of paper and then assign them to treatment groups by pulling their names out of a hat. This illustrates _____.

5. In an experiment, participants in the _____ group do not receive your experimental treatment.

6. In a(n) _____ you expose a group of participants to only one treatment condition.

7. Two types of variables that are often considered in correlational studies are
   _____ and _____.

28

8. Two attributes of a research design that need to be carefully considered during the planning stages are the design's _____ and _____ validity.

9. The presence of confounding variables in an experiment poses a serious threat to _____.

10. The time to be concerned with the internal validity of your experiment is _____ _____.

11. The presence of a(n)_____ interferes with establishing a clear causal connection between your independent and dependent variables.

12. The degree to which results from an experiment generalize to situations beyond the original research situation is called _____.

13. If you were conducting a laboratory experiment to test the validity of a particular theory, you would probably be more concerned with _____, whereas if you were conducting a purely applied experiment you would probably be more concerned with _____.

14. The degree to which a simulation mirrors a real-world phenomenon is _____ _____, whereas the degree to which it psychologically involves participants is _____.

15. An advantage of a field experiment is _____.

Essay Questions

1. Compare and contrast correlational and causal relationships. Give an example of each.

2. Why would it be dangerous to conclude that two variables are causally related based on a correlational study?

3. Discuss the major reasons for using a correlational strategy.

4. Discuss the two defining characteristics of the experimental approach. Why is each important?

5. What are the major advantages and disadvantages of using the experimental approach?

6. Why would you choose field research over laboratory research? What problems might you encounter if you chose field research?

7. What factors must be considered when designing and carrying out a simulation?

EXERCISING YOUR KNOWLEDGE

Weather and Mood: A Correlational Study

Is there a significant relationship between the weather and your mood? This question can be addressed by conducting a simple correlational study. Remember, in a correlational study you collect data on two or more measures and see if they relate significantly to one another. This exercise will introduce you to the basics of conducting a correlational study. To complete this study, do the following:

1. For a 10-day period, collect the information concerning
    a. average temperature,
    b. average barometric pressure,
    c. the amount of sunshine per day (taken as a percentage of the entire day), and
    d. the amount of rainfall.

    You may want to limit the relevant data to the hours that you are awake. So, for example, to obtain the average temperature for a given day you might average the temperature at 9 A.M., noon, 5 P.M., and 10 P.M. Similarly, the average barometric pressure can be obtained. Weather data can be obtained by watching newscasts at the relevant times or by using weather summary tables, printed in most newspapers.

2. Rate your overall mood on each day on a scale ranging from zero to 10 (0 = very bad; 5 = OK; 10 = very good). You might want to create a simple data-coding sheet and keep a record of the relevant data.

3. Once you have collected all your data, you then are in a position to assess the relationship between your weather-related variables and your self-rated mood. To do this use the statistical analysis package that is available from your instructor. Use the "Pearson correlation" subprogram. Alternatively, you can calculate each of the correlations by hand using appropriate statistical formulas available from your instructor.

4. Evaluate the relationship between each of the weather-related variables and your mood measure by answering the following questions:
    a. What were the correlation coefficients obtained?
    b. Were the correlations statistically significant? (This information is provided automatically if you used the program. If you calculated the statistics by hand, you will have to apply a special formula available in just about any introductory statistics text.)
    c. If the correlations were significant, what do they suggest about the relationship between weather and mood? If they were not significant, what conclusions can you draw?
    d. What are the features of this study that make it a correlational study? What kind of inference did you draw about the relationship among the variables (that is, causal or noncausal)? Would it have been possible to answer this question with an experiment? If yes, how? If no, why not?

Identifying Independent and Dependent Variables

In Chapter 3 a distinction was made between independent and dependent variables. In this exercise you are provided with five brief descriptions of published research. Read each carefully and identify the independent variable(s) and dependent variable(s). Also write down the levels of the independent variables identified. Keep in mind that these are brief descriptions. For more information, you should look up the original article and read it.

1. Would you take a drink of water from a fountain if someone were sitting right next to it? In an experiment investigating participants' willingness to violate personal space, Barefoot, Hoople, and McClay (1972) positioned a male or female experimenter near a water fountain. The experimenter was positioned either one foot (near condition) or five feet (far condition) to the right of the fountain or across from the fountain, ten feet away (control condition). The number of people passing the fountain was recorded along with how long a person spent at the fountain if he or she chose to drink. The results showed that fewer participants drank from the fountain in the near condition than in the far or control conditions.

2. Is defensive behavior displayed by many animal species related to the organism's internal motivational state? Davis, Hazelrigg, Moore, and Petty-Zirnstein (1981) investigated factors that affect "defensive burying" behavior of rats. When a rat is exposed to an aversive stimulus (for example, a flash from a flashbulb), the rat will attempt to bury the source of the aversive stimulus. Davis et al. randomly assigned male rats to a food-deprivation, water-deprivation, or no-deprivation condition. Subjects were placed in an experimental chamber and exposed to an aversive stimulus (a bright flash of light from a flashbulb). The amount of time each subject spent in defensive burying behavior and the height of accumulated bedding material (used for burying) were recorded. Results showed that subjects on food or water deprivation engaged in less defensive burying behavior than did nondeprived subjects.

3. Can a student's grades be improved by changing attributions for failure? A study reported by Noel, Forsyth, and Kelley (1987) investigated this question. Students enrolled in an introductory psychology class who had received a *D* or an *F* on the first two exams were randomly assigned to view one of two videotapes. One videotape (attribution tape) depicted two students being interviewed about their academic performance. On this tape the students indicated that they had initially done poorly in school but later improved. They indicated that they stopped blaming external factors (task difficulty, bad teachers, and so on) and began to attribute their performance to internal, controllable factors (such as effort, improving study habits, and seeking help). In the second videotape (nonattribution tape) the students interviewed did not talk about causal attributions for their initial failure and recent success. Instead, they focused on their attitudes and feelings about school. When participants assigned to the two groups were compared, it was found that the participants who saw the attribution tape scored better on the next three exams (75 percent correct) than did those who saw the nonattribution tape (62 percent correct).

4. Parents often use positive reinforcement to increase the frequency of a desired behavior. Does this technique work? Fabes (1987) conducted an experiment to test the effects of reinforcement on children's behavior. Participants were told to build a tower using a set of blocks but to use only the "large blocks" in the set and not the "small blocks." Participants were given either task-contingent reinforcement (children were told that they would receive a small toy when they were done) or performance-contingent reinforcement (children were told that they would receive a small toy only if they built the tower correctly) or they received no promise of reinforcement. The percentage of participants complying immediately with instructions (using only large blocks) and continued interest in using the blocks (percentage of a five-minute observation period after the initial session spent using the blocks) was recorded. The results showed that reinforcement had no significant effect on immediate compliance but that children promised a reward were actually less interested in using the blocks later than were those not promised a reward.

5. If you were asked to do a favor for a relative stranger, would you? Berkowitz (1987) conducted an experiment to investigate some of the factors affecting willingness to help another person. Specifically, Berkowitz was interested in whether or not mood and self-awareness affect willingness to help. A positive, neutral, or negative mood was induced in participants (participants were told to write a paragraph describing a recent incident that made them extremely happy or sad, or an essay on Des Moines, Iowa, to induce the positive, negative, and neutral moods, respectively). Self-awareness was manipulated by having some participants write the essay in front of the reflective surface of a mirror (high awareness) or the nonreflective surface of a mirror (low awareness). After writing the essay and filling out a mood questionnaire, participants were excused from the experiment. Before the participant left, however, the experimenter asked the participant if he or she would be willing to help out by scoring some data sheets. This task involved summing columns of numbers. Berkowitz found that the number of columns that participants summed was affected by both mood and self-awareness. Participants with a positive mood summed more columns ($M = 13.2$) than did participants in a neutral or negative mood ($M = 7.1$ and 2.2, respectively). Participants in the high self-awareness condition summed more columns ($M = 13.85$) than did those in the low self-awareness condition ($M = 8.6$). In addition, self-awareness had the most effect on helping when the participant's mood was positive.

Sources

Barefoot, J. C., Hoople, H., & McClay, D. (1972). Avoidance of an act which would violate personal space. *Psychonomic Science, 28,* 205–206.

Berkowitz, L. (1987). Mood, self-awareness and willingness to help. *Journal of Personality and Social Psychology, 52,* 721–729.

Davis, S. F., Hazelrigg, M., Moore, S. A., & Petty-Zirnstein, M. K. (1981). Defensive burying as a function of food and water deprivation. *Bulletin of the Psychonomic Society, 18,* 325–327.

Fabes, R. A. (1987). Effects of reward contexts on young children's task interest. *Journal of Psychology, 121,* 5–19.

Noel, J. G., Forsyth, D. R., & Kelley, K. N. (1987). Improving test performance of failing students by overcoming their self-serving attributional bias. *Basic and Applied Social Psychology, 8,* 151–162.

Identifying Confounding Variables

Here are two descriptions of published research studies or advertisements (originally discussed by Huck & Sandler, 1979). See if you can detect if any confounding variables exist. For each example, indicate what the confounding is, how it clouds a causal relationship, and offer some tentative solutions for eliminating the confounding.

1. Wexley and Thornton (1972) conducted an experiment to test the hypothesis that providing students with verbal feedback about test results would facilitate learning. During the school term, 169 undergraduate students were given four quizzes. After each quiz participants were reshown 18 of the 35 multiple choice items. The instructor read each of these 18 items, and gave the correct answer and a brief explanation of the correct answer. The instructor indicated that time did not permit going over all 35 items; therefore participants did not see or receive feedback on 17 items per quiz. The final exam in the course consisted of 38 of the feedback questions and 38 of the nonfeedback questions. Wexley and Thornton found that, in general, students did better on items for which feedback was given than those for which feedback was not given. Wexley and Thornton concluded that "the results confirm the assumption that post-test verbal feedback does facilitate learning" (p. 121).

2. In an attempt to show a relationship between anxiety-producing conditions and sexual attraction, Dutton and Aron (1974)* conducted a field experiment. Male participants were approached by either an attractive male or female experimenter and asked to participate in a psychological study on the effects of exposure to scenic attractions on creative expression. Participants were approached at one of two locations. One location was a 450-foot-long footbridge consisting of wooden slats supported by wire cables. This bridge was suspended 230 feet over a canyon (high bridge). The second location was a solid wood bridge 10 feet over a small, shallow river (low bridge). Participants were given an item from the Thematic Apperception Test (TAT) and asked to make up a story about it. After completing the task participants were told that they could receive more information about the study by contacting the experimenter directly. At that point the experimenter tore a small piece of paper from a sheet of paper and wrote his or her telephone number on it and invited the participant to call. The major measure of sexual attraction was the number of participants calling the experimenter for information. The results showed that fewer participants called the male experimenter than called the female and that participants who were approached on the high bridge were more likely to call the female experimenter than those who were approached on the low bridge.

---

* Dutton and Aron were aware of the problem posed in this exercise. In fact, as good researchers will do, they followed up with two subsequent experiments to tease out the possible confounding factors.

Sources

Dutton, D. G., & Aron, A. P. (1974). Some evidence for heightened sexual attraction under conditions of high anxiety. *Journal of Personality and Social Psychology, 30,* 510–517.

Huck, S. W., & Sandler, H. M. (1979). *Rival hypotheses: Alternative explanations of data based conclusions.* New York: Harper & Row.

Wexley, K. N., & Thornton, C. L. (1972). Effect of verbal feedback of test result upon learning. *Journal of Educational Research, 66,* 119–121.

Conducting a Two-Group Experiment

You can demonstrate to yourself how to construct a simple experiment by trying out the following simple experiment on personal space invasion. Personal space is an invisible bubble we carry around us that defines how close we will allow others to approach us. When our personal space is violated we react in a defensive manner, perhaps by backing up. Try the following simple experiment on personal space invasion.

For this experiment approach ten individuals, ostensibly to ask them some questions for a survey you are taking for a class. For half of the participants literally stand toe-to-toe (experimental group) with them and for the other half keep a distance of about two feet (control group). Note the reactions of participants in each group. Your dependent variable could be whether the participant backs away or makes some other defensive move (such as leaning away, folding arms over chest, or looking away). It might be easier to run this experiment in pairs with one person acting as the survey taker and the other an observer measuring the participants' behavior.

After you have completed your experiment summarize your data and determine if you saw more defensive behavior in the experimental group than in the control group. Evaluate your experiment for potential extraneous or confounding variables. What steps did you take to control extraneous variables? What could you have done to make your experiment better or more interesting?

ANSWERS TO QUESTIONS AND EXERCISES

Multiple-Choice Questions

1. A	8. C	15. A
2. B	9. A	16. C
3. D	10. D	17. C
4. D	11. A	18. D
5. C	12. B	19. C
6. D	13. C	20. C
7. A	14. B	21. A

Fill-In Questions

1. the degree of control over variables
2. dependent variable
3. hold them constant across treatments; randomize them across groups

4. randomly assigning participants to groups
5. control
6. demonstration
7. predictor variables; criterion variables
8. internal; external
9. internal validity
10. during the design phase
11. confounding variable
12. external validity
13. internal validity; external validity
14. mundane realism; experimental realism
15. high external validity

Exercising Your Knowledge

Identifying Independent and Dependent Variables

1. *Independent variables:* (1) Distance the experimenter sat from the water fountain (one foot, five feet, or across from the fountain), (2) Sex of experimenter (male or female).

   Dependent variables: Number of participants who stopped to drink and the amount of time spent at the fountain.

2. *Independent variable:* Motivational state of the rat. The levels of the independent variable were food deprived, water deprived, or not deprived.

   Dependent variables: Amount of time spent in defensive burying behavior and the height of bedding material placed over the source of the aversive stimulus.

3. *Independent variable:* The type of interview that the participant saw on the videotape (attributional or nonattributional).

   Dependent variable: Performance on exams after experimental intervention.

4. *Independent variable:* Reinforcement contingency (task contingent, performance contingent, or no reward).

   Dependent variables: (1) Percentage of participants immediately complying with the rules of the task, (2) Percentage of the five-minute observation period that the participant spent playing with the blocks.

5. *Independent variables:* (1) Mood induced (positive, neutral, or negative) by the experimenter, (2) Whether or not participants were made to feel self-aware (mirror or no mirror).

   Dependent variable: Number of columns that participant summed for the experimenter.

Finding the Confounding

1. The confounding variable in problem 1 is that verbal feedback is totally confounded with number of exposures to the items. Recall that participants in the verbal feedback condition were

reshown 18 test items, whereas participants in the nonfeedback condition were not reshown the questions. Could the effect observed be attributed to the fact that some participants were simply exposed more often to the questions than others were?

This confounding cannot be easily eliminated, per se. An additional control group could, however, be added to help rule out the alternative explanation. A third group could be reshown the questions but not be given the feedback and explanation about the correct answer. Comparisons would then be made between the three groups to see just how feedback affects learning.

2. The confounding factor in this experiment, which as we pointed out before was acknowledged by the authors, was a participant selection bias. It could be argued that participants who choose to cross the more dangerous bridge are more the type who would subsequently call an attractive female than participants who choose to cross the safer bridge. Participants who are willing to "take the chance" of crossing the high bridge may, for example, be bolder in general, more arousal seeking, and less inhibited.

Participant selection biases like the one in this problem are not easily eliminated. You could, however, conduct follow-up studies to test the limits of potential alternative explanations. For example, you could have interviewed participants 10 or 15 minutes after they crossed each bridge. If you found no differences in participants' responses, you could be reasonably sure that the original data were not due to selection biases. You could then attribute the observed differences to the arousal actually produced on the bridge. If, on the other hand, participants still differed, then participant selection might still be a problem. In fact, Dutton and Aron (1974) did such follow-up experiments. These experiments support the conclusion that heightened anxiety is related to sexual attraction.

CHAPTER 4

MAKING SYSTEMATIC OBSERVATIONS

KEY QUESTIONS TO CONSIDER

- What factors should you consider when deciding what to observe in a study?
- What is the reliability of a measure?
- How does the concept of reliability apply to different types of measures?
- What is meant by the accuracy of a measure?
- How do the reliability and accuracy of a measure affect the generality of a study?
- What is the validity of a measure?
- What are the ways you can assess the validity of a measure?
- What is the relationship between the validity and reliability of a measure?
- What information about a measure is conveyed by each of Stevens's four "scales of measurement"? Do all measures fall neatly into one of those categories?
- What factors should be considered when choosing a scale of measurement?
- What is ecological validity and why should you be concerned about it?
- What is meant by the adequacy of a dependent measure?
- What two problems affect the adequacy of a dependent variable?
- Under what conditions would you consider tailoring your dependent measures to your research participants?
- What are the defining characteristics of the three types of dependent variables? What are the advantages and disadvantages of each?
- How can the act of measurement affect responses?
- What are role attitude cues, and how might they affect your study?
- What are demand characteristics and experimenter bias?
- What techniques can you use to reduce reactivity in research?
- What are pilot studies and why are they used?
- What are manipulation checks and why should you include them in your research?

CHAPTER OUTLINE

REVIEW AND STUDY QUESTIONS

Key Term Definition

Define each of the following terms.

Reliability:

Test–retest reliability:

Parallel forms reliability:

Split-half reliability:

Accuracy:

Validity:

Face validity:

Content validity:

Criterion-related validity:

Concurrent validity:

Predictive validity:

Construct validity:

Nominal scale:

Ordinal scale:

Interval scale:

Ratio scale:

Range effects:

Behavioral measure:

Physiological measure:

Self-report measure:

Demand characteristics:

Role attitude cues:

Experimenter bias:

Expectancy effects:

Single-blind:

Double-blind:

Pilot study:

Manipulation checks:

Multiple-Choice Questions

Circle the alternative that best completes the stem of each question.

1. Your choice of specific variables to observe in a study may depend on
    a. research tradition.
    b. theory.
    c. availability of new techniques or equipment.
    d. any of the above

2. If a measure is able to produce similar results when it is used repeatedly under identical conditions it is said to be
   a. valid.
   b. reliable.
   c. precise.
   d. error free.

3. The precision of a measure refers to
   a. the range of variation expected on repeated measurement.
   b. whether the measure produces the same results under identical conditions.
   c. whether the measure measures what you intend it to measure.
   d. how well subjects can understand the measure and use it correctly.
   e. none of the above

4. To measure the reliability of judgments of multiple observers you would use a statistical measure of
   a. precision.
   b. margin of error.
   c. interrater reliability.
   d. interobserver concordance.

5. A technique for assessing reliability of a measure in which a test is administered more than once is known as _____.
   a. multiple test reliability
   b. repeated testing reliability
   c. parallel forms reliability
   d. test–retest reliability

6. Nonequivalence of test items is most likely to be a problem for which method of testing reliability?
   a. Parallel forms reliability
   b. Split-half reliability
   c. Test–retest reliability
   d. both a and b
   e. both b and c

7. If the results of a measure agree with a known standard, the measure is said to be
   a. valid.
   b. reliable.
   c. accurate.
   d. precise.

8. Just because a measure is reliable, it does not guarantee that it is
   a. accurate.
   b. valid.
   c. useful.
   d. all of the above
   e. both a and b

9. The extent to which a measure measures what you intend it to measure is known as the
   _____ of that measure.
   a. precision
   b. accuracy
   c. validity
   d. reliability

10. If a new measure you have developed produces results similar to those provided by an established measure of the same variable, your new measure is said to show
    a. criterion-related validity.
    b. predictive validity.
    c. parallel forms reliability.
    d. accuracy and precision.

11. According to the text, _____ validity is the weakest form of validity.
    a. face
    b. content
    c. predictive
    d. concurrent

12. According to the text, which of the following is true?
    a. If a measure is reliable it must be valid.
    b. A measure can be reliable but be invalid.
    c. If a measure is reliable it must be accurate.
    d. If a measure is precise it must be valid.

13. An independent variable consists of four types of treatment for drug dependency. The variable falls along a(n) _____ scale.
    a. nominal
    b. ordinal
    c. interval
    d. ratio

14. If a measure falls along a ratio scale,
    a. the ordering of values is meaningless.
    b. the zero point of the scale is arbitrary.
    c. a zero value indicates the absence of the scaled quantity.
    d. you can only rank-order the values.

15. The scale that provides the most information about a variable is the _____ scale.
    a. nominal
    b. ordinal
    c. interval
    d. ratio

16. When selecting an appropriate statistic to summarize or analyze a set of numbers, you
    a. need only to determine which of Stevens's scales of measurement applies.
    b. must consider how the numbers were used.
    c. can use any statistic you prefer.
    d. none of the above

17. When it is necessary to use a less informative scale in order to preserve ecological validity, you can do so while gaining the information provided by a higher scale if you
    a. conduct a parametric analysis of the less informative scale data.
    b. conduct a nonparametric analysis of the less informative scale data.
    c. use a composite scale that combines the features of both scales.
    d. use the higher scale and then rescale the data to the less informative scale.

18. Observation may fail to reveal the effect of an independent variable if the dependent variable
    a. lacks adequate sensitivity.
    b. correlates strongly with the independent variable.
    c. fails to show either a floor or ceiling effect.
    d. all of the above

19. A range effect may
    a. reduce the differences among your treatment means.
    b. reduce the variability of scores within treatments.
    c. produce misleading results when you conduct a statistical analysis of the data.
    d. all of the above

20. This technique used with preverbal children capitalizes on the fact that even infants get bored with repeatedly presented stimuli.
    a. preference technique
    b. habituation
    c. discrimination learning
    d. classical conditioning

21. Special equipment designed to measure the subject's bodily responses is used to collect _____ measures.
    a. behavioral
    b. physiological
    c. self-report
    d. psychophysical

22. For the human participant, the psychological experiment is a
    a. lark.
    b. waste of time.
    c. social situation.
    d. traumatic experience.

23. Cues provided by the researcher and the experimental situation can communicate to the participant the purpose of the study and expected responses. Such cues are termed
    a. demand characteristics.
    b. experimenter bias.
    c. expectation bias.
    d. observer contamination.

24. Participants who come into a psychological experiment worried about what will happen to them exhibit a(n) _____ attitude.
    a. cooperative
    b. defensive or apprehensive
    c. negative
    d. uncooperative

25. Experimenter bias may emerge in the results when
    a. the experimenter develops preconceived ideas about the capacities of the participants.
    b. participants in different experimental conditions are not treated identically (except for the level of the independent variable, of course).
    c. either a or b
    d. participants are biased either for or against the experimenter.

26. One way to help eliminate experimenter bias is to
    a. automate the experiment.
    b. prevent the participants from learning what condition of the experiment they are in.
    c. make specific predictions concerning the expected outcome of the experiment.
    d. all of the above

27. When you use animal subjects in your experiments,
    a. you do not have to worry about demand characteristics.
    b. you do not have to worry about experimenter bias.
    c. blind techniques for conducting the experiment are not effective.
    d. none of the above

28. Automating your experiments
    a. reduces the influence of experimenter bias.
    b. can save time, because equipment such as computers can be used in many cases to actually conduct the experiment.
    c. increases the precision of your experiment.
    d. all of the above

Fill-In Questions

Fill in the blanks with the word or phrase that best completes each sentence.

1. If your research question follows up on previous research, your decision about what to observe may be determined by _____.

2. If repeated measurements made under identical conditions give the same result, the measure is said to be _____.

3. The precision of an estimate of a population mean from a sample is known as _____.

4. The degree of agreement among several observers of the same measure provides a measure of _____ reliability.

5. When assessing the reliability of a measure one can administer the measure twice and then correlate the two sets of scores. The measure is reliable when the correlation is _____.

6. _____ is assessed by combining two forms of the same measure in a single test.

7. A measure that is _____ produces results that agree with a known standard.

8. If a measure lacks _____, then it fails to measure what it was intended to measure.

9. If a test adequately samples behavior it is said to have _____ validity.

10. If the scores on a new measure correlate highly with scores on another established measure administered at about the same time, your measure has _____ validity.

11. Phrenology failed as a science because, as measures of temperament and ability, the phrenologists' measures were _____.

12. Dividing one value by another gives meaningful results only if the value has been measured on a(n) _____ scale.

13. Values measured on a(n) _____ scale can be rank-ordered, but the distance between values is not known.

14. A measure is said to be _____ valid if it reflects what people must do in real-life situations.

45

15. If your measurements in various conditions of an experiment remain at or near the top of the scale, variability in scores is restricted by this _____ effect.

16. A count of the number of behavioral responses over time gives the _____ of responding.

17. In the _____ verbal report, participants speculate on how they would react in a certain future situation.

18. When designing experiments, the _____ nature of human participants must be taken into account.

19. Demand characteristics of an experiment that signal what attitude is needed in order to conform to the role of research subject are called _____ cues.

20. _____ effects emerge when the experimenter has preconceived ideas about the capacities of the participants.

21. If neither the participant nor the person conducting the experiment knows which treatment condition the participant is in, a(n) _____ technique is being used.

22. You can increase the accuracy and reliability of your measurements, save time, and reduce experimenter effects by _____ your experiment.

23. You can connect a computer to other equipment, such as operant chambers, by means of a(n) _____.

24. A(n) _____ study is conducted to test the adequacy of your materials, measures, and procedure.

25. To determine whether your independent variables have their intended effects on your participants, your design should include _____.

Essay Questions

1. Identify four factors that may influence your choice of specific variables to observe and manipulate. Briefly describe each.

2. How could you demonstrate that a measure is reliable and that it is accurate?

3. List the pros and cons of using an established measure versus a new one.

4. If you encounter a ceiling effect with a particular measure, what could you do to correct the problem?

5. List three broad categories of dependent measure, and provide specific types under each.

6. Describe the sources of bias in an experiment that result from the reactive nature of psychological measurement.

EXERCISING YOUR KNOWLEDGE

Accuracy of Measurement

Draw several lines of different lengths on a sheet of paper (make at least 20 lines, from very short to nearly the width of the paper). Estimate the length of each line in millimeters and write this estimate under the line. Then use a ruler (the type with a millimeter scale on one side) to get the actual lengths to the nearest millimeter. Write this number next to your estimates. Now plot your estimates on the graph on the next page. Using the ruler, draw a straight line that seems to provide the best eyeball "fit" to the data points. How well did your estimates agree with the true lengths? Your estimates are unreliable to the extent that they deviate from the straight line. Were your estimates reasonably reliable? Your estimates were accurate (on the average) to the extent that the line falls on the leading diagonal (points 0,0; 50,50; 200,200; and so on). Draw this diagonal and compare it to your estimated line. How well do the two lines agree? In what ways do they deviate?

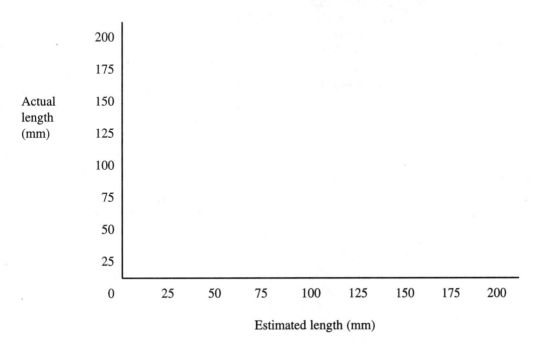

ANSWERS TO QUESTIONS AND EXERCISES

Multiple-Choice Questions

1.	D	11.	A	21.	B
2.	B	12.	B	22.	C
3.	A	13.	A	23.	A
4.	C	14.	C	24.	B
5.	D	15.	D	25.	C
6.	D	16.	B	26.	A
7.	C	17.	C	27.	D
8.	D	18.	A	28.	D
9.	C	19.	D		
10.	A	20.	B		

Fill-In Questions

1.	research tradition	15.	ceiling
2.	reliable	16.	frequency
3.	margin of error	17.	prospective
4.	interrater	18.	reactive
5.	high	19.	role attitude
6.	Split-half reliability	20.	Expectancy
7.	accurate	21.	double-blind
8.	validity	22.	automating
9.	content	23.	interface
10.	concurrent	24.	pilot
11.	invalid	25.	manipulation checks
12.	ratio		
13.	ordinal		
14.	ecologically		

CHAPTER 5

CHOOSING AND USING SUBJECTS

KEY QUESTIONS TO CONSIDER

- What factors affect your decision to use animal subjects or human participants?
- What is a population and how does it relate to a sample?
- What is a sample and how is it used in research?
- What is random sampling and how does it affect the generality of your research?
- What is nonrandom sampling and how does it relate to the generality of your research?
- Under what conditions is random sampling preferred over nonrandom sampling?
- Why did the APA code of research ethics evolve?
- What are the historical roots of the APA code of research ethics?
- What are the main points contained in the APA code of research ethics?
- What role does the institutional review board play in research?
- How can ethical guidelines affect how you conduct and interpret your research?
- How does the nature of your research affect how you will acquire human participants?
- How does the requirement of voluntary participation affect the validity of your research?
- How do participant characteristics and situational factors relate to one's decision to volunteer for research?
- How can volunteerism affect the internal and external validity of your research?
- What can you do to reduce the problem of volunteerism in research?
- What is deception in research and when is it allowed?
- What effect does deception have on your participants?
- What solutions are there to the problem of deception? What are the advantages and disadvantages of each solution?
- Why would you consider using animals as subjects in your research?
- What affects your decision about which animal to use in research and how can the chosen animal be obtained?
- What ethical guidelines must you follow when using animals as subjects in research?
- Must the results from animal research generalize to humans? Why or why not?

- What arguments have animal rights activists made against using animals in research? How have scientists addressed the issues raised by animal rights activists?
- What alternatives to using animals in research have been proposed? What are the advantages and disadvantages of those techniques?

CHAPTER OUTLINE

Using Subjects: General Considerations
    Populations and Samples
    Sampling and Generalization
    Is Random Sampling Always Necessary?
Considerations When Using Human Participants
    Ethical Research Practice
        Nazi War Crimes and the Nuremberg Code
        APA Ethical Guidelines
        Government Regulations
    Ethical Guidelines, Your Research, and the IRB
Acquiring Human Participants for Research
    The Research Setting
        Laboratory Research
        Field Research
    The Needs of Your Research
    Institutional Policies and Ethical Guidelines
Voluntary Participation and Validity
    Factors That Affect the Decision to Volunteer
        Participant-Related Characteristics
        Situational Factors
    Volunteerism and Internal Validity
    Volunteerism and External Validity
    Remedies for Volunteerism
Research Using Deception
    Solutions to the Problem of Deception
        Role Playing
        Obtaining Prior Consent to Be Deceived
        Debriefing
Considerations When Using Animals as Subjects in Research
    Contributions of Research Using Animal Subjects
    Choosing Which Animal to Use
    Why Use Animals?
    How to Acquire Animals for Research
    Ethical Considerations
    Should the Research Be Done?

REVIEW AND STUDY QUESTIONS

Key Term Definition

Define each of the following terms.

Population:

Sample:

Generalization:

Random sample:

Nonrandom sample:

Institutional review board (IRB):

Volunteer bias:

Deception:

Role playing:

Debriefing:

Institutional animal care and use committee (IACUC):

Multiple-Choice Questions

Circle the alternative that best completes the stem of each question.

1. The large group of individuals from which you select a smaller group to include in your experiment is the
   a. sample.
   b. population.
   c. target group.
   d. experimental group.

2. If each individual has an equal chance of being chosen for your experiment, then your sample is classified as
   a. general.
   b. stratified.
   c. random.
   d. biased.

3. According to your text, most experiments in psychology use a
   a. nonrandom sample.
   b. random sample.
   c. general sample.
   d. stratified sample.

4. The generality of your research results is affected by
   a. how representative your sample is of the population.
   b. how realistic your research setting is.
   c. how your independent variables are manipulated.
   d. all of the above
   e. both a and b only

5. According to the text, the highest level of generality will result from research using a
   a. nonrandom sample.
   b. true random sample.
   c. strategy combining nonrandom and random sampling.
   d. stratified sample.

6. If you want to apply your research results directly to a population, then it is especially crucial to use a
   a. nonrandom sample.
   b. subject pool.
   c. random sample.
   d. systematic sample.

7. According to the text, true random sampling is less of a concern in most psychological research because
   a. we are not interested in generalizing our results.
   b. nonrandom sampling is actually superior to random sampling when it comes to the generality of results.
   c. we often directly apply our results to a population.
   d. the goal of most psychological research is to make predictions from a theory to specific behavior.

8. Which of the following is *not* one of the APA ethical guidelines for use of human participants in research?
   a. Participation in research must be voluntary.
   b. Participants must have the right to decline participation at any time.
   c. Participants cannot be paid for their service in research.
   d. Participants must be informed of any aspects of the experiment that might affect their decision to participate.

9. Before you can run your research, an IRB reviews your research to make sure that
   a. participants are treated according to accepted ethical standards.
   b. you do not have any extraneous variables in your study that could confound your results.
   c. your sample is truly random.
   d. all of the above

10. According to Rosenthal and Rosnow (1975), we can have maximum confidence that volunteers tend to _____ than nonvolunteers.
    a. be of higher intelligence
    b. come from a higher social class
    c. be more social
    d. all of the above

11. Research shows that participants are more likely to volunteer for an experiment if
    a. they are not offered any external rewards for participation.
    b. they are interested in the topic being studied in the research.
    c. the experiment is highly stressful.
    d. none of the above

12. Horowitz (1969) conducted an experiment testing the impact of voluntary participation on attitude change. Based on his findings we could conclude that
    a. voluntary participation does not appear to be a major problem.
    b. voluntary participation affects the results of an experiment only when the experiment involves high levels of stress or boredom.
    c. volunteer and nonvolunteer participants react very differently to experimental manipulations.
    d. nonvolunteer participants are less influenced by experimental manipulations than are volunteer participants.

13. According to Rosenthal and Rosnow (1975),
    a. little can be done about the problem of voluntary participation affecting the outcome of research.
    b. the impact of volunteerism can be reduced only if all your participants are female because most females volunteer for research anyway.
    c. the impact of volunteerism can be reduced by using a power-assertive approach to recruitment.
    d. none of the above

14. Which of the following is *not* an example of active deception?
    a. making false promises to participants
    b. making concealed observations of participants
    c. misrepresenting the true purposes of research
    d. using pseudoparticipants

15. According to Holmes (1976), a negative side effect of using deception is
    a. reduced internal validity of research.
    b. that because participants have been duped by an experimenter they may experience a loss of self-esteem.
    c. that participants may actually bend over backward to please an experimenter in a subsequent study.
    d. none of the above

16. After an experiment using deception, participants should be told of the deception and the reasons for it. This is known as
    a. debriefing.
    b. dehoaxing.
    c. desensitizing.
    d. deflating.

17. According to the text,
    a. research using animal subjects is of little use because the results rarely generalize to humans.
    b. the worth of research using animals should not be judged according to whether or not results generalize to humans.
    c. although research using animal subjects can be used to answer some interesting basic questions, it cannot be used to develop models relevant to human behavior.
    d. research using animal subjects is usually cruel and should be eliminated.

18. Which of the following is a good reason to consider using animals in research?
    a. Some procedures can be used only on animal subjects.
    b. You can exert greater control over experimental and living conditions than you can with humans.
    c. You need not worry about adhering to ethical guidelines when you use animal subjects.
    d. both a and b
    e. all of the above

19. When considering whether research using animal subjects should be done, researchers must consider
    a. the cost of the study to the animals weighed against its potential benefits.
    b. the likelihood that the I-knew-it-all-along effect will occur.
    c. only the importance of the potential contributions of the study.
    d. only how the animals will be affected by the research.

20. According to the text, who should be on a committee to review proposals for animal research?
    a. A veterinarian trained in laboratory animal science or medicine
    b. A member of the public not affiliated with animal research or the sponsoring institution
    c. A practicing scientist who does animal research
    d. all of the above
    e. both a and b only

21. Methods that substitute tissue cultures for whole organisms are called _____ methods.
    a. simulation
    b. *in vivo*
    c. *in vitro*
    d. de novo

Fill-In Questions

Fill in the blanks with the word or phrase that best completes each sentence.

1. _____ is a term referring to how well the results from an experiment apply to the population.

2. According to research by Higbee, Millard, and Folkman (1982), most human participants used in psychological research are _____.

3. Present-day ethical guidelines are strongly rooted in the _____, which was established after World War II.

4. A(n)_____ explains research to participants and is read and signed by participants prior to participation in research.

5. For most laboratory experiments, participants are acquired from a(n) _____ _____.

6. A common practice used to acquire human participants for research was _____ _____, which is now unethical.

7. In a field experiment you typically have _____ over participant selection than you have in a laboratory experiment.

8. The characteristics of participants who volunteer for research may affect how they perform in an experiment. This problem is called _____.

9. According to Holmes (1976a, b), participants exposed to deception in research should be _____ and _____.

10. Research shows that the problem of using volunteer participants in research affects the _____ of an experiment.

11. Unrecognized conditioning and participant observation are examples of _____ _____.

12. An alternative to deception that involves informing participants about all aspects of the research and asking participants to act as though they were exposed to a treatment is _____.

13. Using demonstrations, allowing participants to watch subsequent experimental sessions, and making participants active participants in research are all ways to _____ _____.

14. Rats are the most popular animals used as subjects in research because _____ _____.

15. According to Singer (1975), it is _____ to set humans above other animal species.

Essay Questions

1. Outline the procedures you would follow when acquiring a sample of subjects for a research project of your own choosing. What factors must you consider when selecting your sample?

2. Discuss the issue of random and nonrandom sampling in psychological research. In your answer address the issues of when random sampling is necessary and why nonrandom sampling may not always be necessary. Also discuss how random and nonrandom sampling affect generality.

3. Compare and contrast the differences inherent in acquiring participants for laboratory and field research. How are internal and external validity affected?

4. How does the requirement that participants be volunteers affect the outcome of an experiment? How can some of the effects of volunteerism be reduced?

5. Imagine that you are going to conduct an experiment that requires deception. How can you justify the use of deception and what steps would you take to reduce the impact of deception on your participants?

6. Describe how a proposal for using animals in research would be reviewed to ensure ethical treatment of the animal subjects. Who would be on the committee to review such applications and why do you think they should be on the committee?

7. Some individuals in the animal rights movement advocate that animals not be used in research. Why is such a radical approach not tenable for the science of psychology?

EXERCISING YOUR KNOWLEDGE

Evaluating Research for Ethical Considerations

The literature abounds with examples of research where ethical principles may have been violated. Here are three examples from the research literature. For each example, do the following:

- Identify what you think is an ethical violation.
- Refer to the Ethical Principles of the APA listed in Chapter 5, and indicate which principle(s) you think the research violates.
- Recommend a solution to the ethical violation. That is, what could the researchers have done to reduce the ethical problem(s) inherent in the research example?

1. Middlemist, Knowles, and Matter (1976) conducted a study investigating whether or not invasions of personal space are physiologically as well as psychologically arousing. The experiment was run in a men's lavatory. By closing off one or another urinal, participants were forced to urinate either in the urinal next to a male confederate of the experimenter or in the urinal one away from the confederate. A second confederate was positioned (so to speak) in a toilet stall adjacent to the urinals. Using a periscope the second confederate observed the urination behavior of the participants. The latency to onset of urination and duration of onset of urination were recorded by the observer.

2. In a classic experiment on cognitive dissonance theory, Festinger and Carlsmith (1959) had participants engage in an extremely boring task. After doing this task, participants were asked if they would help out in the experiment with the next participant because the regular assistant did not show up. The accomplice-participants were asked to tell the next participant that the task was really interesting and exciting. For telling this little white lie the accomplice-participant was told that he would be paid (either $1 or $20, depending on the condition to

which he was assigned). The experiment was actually designed to see if the amount of money promised affected the accomplice-participant's attitude toward the boring task. At the end of the experiment participants were asked to return the money that they had been paid.

3. In a simulation study of plea bargaining, Gregory, Mowen, and Linder (1978) gave false feedback to undergraduate participants. Participants waited in a waiting room for an experiment to begin. In one condition another participant who had just been in the experiment (actually a confederate of the experimenter) told the waiting participant that most of the answers to the test that would be taken were "B." In a second condition no information was given to the waiting participant. After the participant took the tests the experimenter accused the participant of cheating and told him it was a serious matter that would have to be presented to a review board for action. Participants were led to believe that the consequences of the accused cheating were very severe. The participants were told that if they admitted cheating they would simply lose credit for participating in the experiment.

Sources

Festinger, L., & Carlsmith, J. M. (1959). Cognitive consequences of forced compliance. *Journal of Abnormal and Social Psychology, 58,* 203–210.

Gregory, W. L., Mowen, J. C., & Linder, D. E. (1978). Social psychology and plea bargaining: Applications, methodology and theory. *Journal of Personality and Social Psychology, 36,* 1521–1530.

Middlemist, R. D., Knowles, E. S., & Matter, C. F. (1976). Personal space invasions in the lavatory: Suggestive evidence for arousal. *Journal of Personality and Social Psychology, 33,* 541–546.

How Are Animals Used in Research?

Go to your university's library and find two articles in which animals were used as subjects (such articles can be found in the *Journal of the Experimental Analysis of Behavior, Journal of Experimental Psychology,* and the *Journal of Comparative and Physiological Psychology*). For each article, answer the following:

1. How were the subjects obtained, housed, and treated by the researchers?

2. Did the research methodology adhere to the ethical guidelines specified in Chapter 5 of the text?

3. Could the research have been done using either *in vitro* or computer simulation methods? If so, how?

ANSWERS TO QUESTIONS AND EXERCISES

Multiple-Choice Questions

1.	B	12.	C
2.	C	13.	D
3.	A	14.	B
4.	D	15.	B
5.	B	16.	A
6.	C	17.	B
7.	D	18.	D
8.	C	19.	A
9.	A	20.	D
10.	D	21.	C
11.	B		

Fill-In Questions

1. Generalization
2. college students
3. Nuremberg Code
4. informed consent form
5. participant pool
6. required participation
7. less control
8. volunteer bias
9. dehoaxed; desensitized
10. internal and external validity
11. passive deception
12. role playing
13. increase the effectiveness of debriefing
14. of cost or of ease of handling and housing
15. species-ist

Exercising Your Knowledge

Evaluating Research for Ethical Problems

1.   The problem with the Middlemist, Knowles, and Matter investigation is that it could be argued that the participant's privacy was invaded by the experimenters. Is it ethical to observe and record a "private behavior" like urination even if it takes place in a public restroom? In addition, no informed consent was obtained from participants.

   The difficulties presented by this study are not easy to eliminate. It might be justifiable to invade a participant's privacy in the name of science. Obtaining informed consent prior to exposing participants to the experimental manipulations would, obviously, bias the results terribly. As an alternative you might consider having another experimenter outside the restroom. This experimenter could stop the participant, explain the fact that he was just in an experiment, inform him of the purpose of the experiment, and obtain informed consent *after* the participant has been exposed to the experimental treatment. Data from participants who do not agree to having their data included would be deleted.

2. There are two problems with this study. First, participants were deceived into believing that they would be paid money for their assistance to the experimenter. Later the money was taken back. Second, participants were asked to tell a lie to another participant. This may lead to lowering of a participant's self-esteem. The participant may find out that he or she is "the type of person who would lie for money."

One solution to the problem of taking back the money is to let participants keep the promised money. This may not be possible, however, especially if you do not have a grant to pay participants. As an alternative, participants should be carefully debriefed and *asked* to return the money. The debriefing could include an explanation that it was necessary to offer the money to test the hypotheses and that the money is needed for other participants in the same experiment. Participants would probably cooperate and return the money. Debriefing could also be used to reduce the ill effects of the lie telling. Participants should be told that they behaved in much the same way as other participants and that their behavior is by no means abnormal.

3. The potential problem raised in the Gregory, Mowen, and Linder study is that participants are placed in a highly stressful situation believing that they were "caught cheating" and were in trouble. There is no way to avoid the arousal of stress. However, you could (as suggested in the text) have participants read and sign an informed consent form indicating that the experiment in which they will participate may involve stress, without specifying the source of the stress.

CHAPTER 6

USING NONEXPERIMENTAL DESIGNS

KEY QUESTIONS TO CONSIDER

- What are the defining characteristics of observational research?
- How do observational techniques apply to both nonexperimental and experimental research?
- How are behavioral categories used in observational research developed?
- What are the major techniques used to make behavioral observations in observational research?
- What is the distinction between recording single events and behavior sequences?
- What are the sampling techniques used to handle complexity in observational research?
- Why and how would you evaluate interrater reliability?
- How do you deal with data from multiple observers?
- What are the sources of bias in observational research and what techniques can be used to reduce it?
- What is the difference between quantitative and qualitative data? What are the problems inherent in collecting qualitative data?
- What are naturalistic observation and unobtrusive observation? How are they used to study behavior?
- What are some of the advantages and disadvantages of naturalistic observation?
- What is ethnography and what are some of the important issues facing a field ethnographer?
- How are data recorded and analyzed in ethnography?
- What are the defining characteristics of sociometry? In what capacities can sociometry be used?
- How are the case history method and archival research used?
- What is content analysis and what steps are taken when using it?

CHAPTER OUTLINE

Conducting Observational Research
    Developing Behavioral Categories
    Quantifying Behavior in an Observational Study
        Frequency Method

REVIEW AND STUDY QUESTIONS

Key Term Definition

Define each of the following terms.

Behavioral categories:

Interrater reliability:

Qualitative data:

Naturalistic observation:

Ethnography:

Participant observation:

Nonparticipant observation:

Sociometry:

Sociogram:

Case history:

Archival research:

Content analysis:

Multiple-Choice Questions

Circle the alternative that best completes the stem of each question.

1. _____ are the general and specific classes of behavior you are interested in observing.
   a. Behavioral categories
   b. Sampling categories
   c. Observational categories
   d. Rating categories

2. During an observational study of play behavior among preschoolers, Dr. Smith observes only one behavior and records all instances of that behavior. The method Dr. Smith is using is
   a. time sampling.
   b. individual sampling.
   c. recording behavior sequences.
   d. event sampling.

3. Because Dr. Smith is observing complex behavior, she cannot observe all of her participants at once. Instead, she selects a certain child, observes him for a few minutes, and observes another child for a few minutes. This process is continued until she observes all of her participants several times. Dr. Smith is using
   a. time sampling.
   b. event sampling.
   c. individual sampling.
   d. participant sampling.

4. An advantage of recording behavior sequences is that
   a. the behaviors recorded are less complex than if single behaviors are recorded.
   b. a more complete picture of complex behavior is obtained.
   c. multiple observers are not needed.
   d. all of the above

5. An advantage of using recording instead of live observations is that
   a. recording allows you to review your participants' behavior several times.
   b. multiple observers can conveniently watch and code your participants' behavior.
   c. a camera may be more easily hidden than a live observer.
   d. all of the above

6. Multiple observers are used to
   a. establish the reliability of observations.
   b. relieve fatigue.
   c. ensure the validity of observations.
   d. none of the above

7. Cohen's Kappa is a statistic used to
   a. simplify data from an observational study.
   b. establish if your behavioral categories are valid.
   c. estimate the amount of interrater reliability.
   d. none of the above

8. When using Cohen's Kappa, the first step is to summarize data in a(n)
   a. validity matrix.
   b. observer matrix.
   c. contingency matrix.
   d. confusion matrix.

9. According to your text, a Cohen's Kappa of _____ is acceptable.
   a. .3
   b. .5
   c. .7
   d. 1.00

10. When dealing with data from multiple observers, you can
    a. average across observers if there is a high level of agreement.
    b. designate one observer as the "main" observer prior to beginning your study and use the other to establish reliability.
    c. designate the observer that produces data that confirm your hypothesis as the main observer.
    d. both a and b
    e. all of the above

11. Observer bias may occur if
    a. your observers know the hypotheses of your study.
    b. observers interpret what they see rather than simply record behavior.
    c. your observers are blind to the purposes of your study.
    d. both a and b

12. For his dissertation a graduate student is interested in studying interpersonal interaction distances among couples who have just met. He goes to several local bars and waits until a male approaches a female to make conversation. He then quantifies interaction distance by estimating the distance between them. The research approach he is using is
    a. naturalistic observation.
    b. participant observation.
    c. a field experiment.
    d. none of the above

13. According to the text, a disadvantage of naturalistic observation is that it
    a. does not allow you to carefully observe the behavior of your subjects.
    b. does not allow you to determine the causes of behavior.
    c. is time consuming and expensive.
    d. both a and b
    e. both b and c

14. A research technique in which you make careful observations and record the social structure of a group is known as
    a. sociometry.
    b. a case study.
    c. ethnography.
    d. content analysis.

15. Leslie is studying a cult group by joining the group and making careful observations of how the group functions. Leslie is using _____ to do her research.
    a. participant observation
    b. nonparticipant observation
    c. blind observation
    d. archival research

16. One way to overcome the problem of observers influencing the behavior of subjects being observed is to
    a. train participant observers not to interfere with the normal behavior of subjects.
    b. have participant observers become passive observers.
    c. use covert observation.
    d. all of the above
    e. both a and b only

17. Which of the following would you do if you were conducting an ethnographic study of a group?
    a. Carefully quantify as many behaviors as possible.
    b. Make qualitative field notes that you will transcribe at the end of the day.
    c. Avoid interacting with members of the group.
    d. All of the above

18. Jorge goes into a day care center and has children indicate which other children they like the most and least to see who is the most popular and least popular child. Jorge is using
    a. participant observation.
    b. ethnography.
    c. sociometry.
    d. content analysis.

19. According to the text, which of the following is true of sociometry?
    a. It can be used as a stand-alone research tool.
    b. It can be used in a study as one of several measures.
    c. It is rarely used as a stand-alone research tool.
    d. both a and b
    e. both b and c

20. In a content analysis of children's literature you look for instances in which females and males are portrayed in nonstereotyped ways. These instances would be classified as
    a. context units.
    b. recording units.
    c. content units.
    d. behavioral units.

Fill-In Questions

Fill in the blanks with the word or phrase that best completes each sentence.

1. Two ways to develop valid behavioral categories for behavioral research are _____ _____ and _____.

2. In an observational study of children's play, you record which behaviors follow one another. You are recording _____.

3. A method of quantifying behavior in which you scan your participants for a specific amount of time is _____.

4. In _____ you insinuate yourself into a group and make observations.

5. The case history method can be used to _____ or _____.

6. List two disadvantages of archival research: _____ and _____.

7. When doing a content analysis, you should record both _____ _____ and _____.

8. To avoid observer bias in content analysis, it is a good idea to use _____ _____.

9. Written records of behavior that comprise the data from an experiment are known as _____ data.

10. _____ is a research technique that is used primarily to study and describe the functioning of groups through a study of social interactions or expressions between people.

11. In _____ you observe behavior, but do not become a part of a group being studied.

12. Your first task when conducting an ethnographic study is to_____.

13. The first step in analyzing data from an ethnographic study is to _____.

14. _____ is a research technique that involves identifying and measuring interpersonal relationships within a group.

15. Data from a sociometric study are often plotted graphically on a(n) _____.

16. In a(n) _____ you observe and report on a single case.

17. Archival research makes use of _____ as its source of data.

18. If you wanted to analyze the speeches made by the president, most likely you would use

_____.

19. The unit of analysis, or material you analyze, in a content analysis is known as the

_____

Essay Questions

1. Imagine that you are interested in doing an observational study of the behaviors of preteens at a dance. Outline how you would go about conducting such a study. Be sure to define what your behavioral categories would be and how you would make your observations.

2. Discuss the procedures used for establishing interrater reliability.

3. Discuss the advantages and disadvantages of conducting naturalistic observation.

4. Describe and discuss the five "steps" involved in conducting an ethnographic study. What special issues do you face at each step?

5. You are interested in studying the patterns of social interactions among members of a youth group. Show how you would use sociometric techniques to conduct your study.

6. Outline how you would conduct a content analysis of the amount of violence in children's cartoon programming. What would your recording unit be, and how would you make your observations?

EXERCISING YOUR KNOWLEDGE

Naturalistic Observation

One of the research methods discussed in Chapter 6 of the text is naturalistic observation. This involves watching subjects in their natural environment and recording ongoing behavior. For this exercise you will conduct a limited naturalistic observation study. The first thing you need to do is to decide on the behavior(s) that you will observe. Some suggestions are

A. If you have a zoo nearby, you could select an animal species (for example, monkeys, apes, lions, and so on) for observation.

B. Call a local day care center and see if you can get permission to observe children during free-play hours.

C. Go to a local shopping mall and observe shoppers at a particular location.

After you have selected a behavior, you must then decide how to make your observations. You will have to determine the method after you have decided on who will be observed and where the observations are to be made. If you are going to watch animals in a zoo or children in a day care center, then you may want to use individual sampling. On the other hand, if you opt for watching people in a shopping mall, you may want to choose a location (for example, near a skating rink, outside a particular store) and observe the types of behaviors observed across individuals.

Regardless of what you choose you must clearly define the behaviors that you will record. For example, if you are watching children in a day care center, you may want to include aggressive behavior, solitary play, social play, helping, and so on. If you are watching in a mall, then you may want to record how many participants pass by the store, stop to look in the window, and go into the store. Once you have decided on the behaviors to observe, then make a coding sheet like the one shown in Figure 6-1 in your text. On the day that you are going to make your observations, position yourself in an inconspicuous place and record behavior for thirty minutes (broken down into thirty, 1-minute intervals).

Data Analysis and Evaluation of Your Methodology

To analyze your data, do the following:

1. For each of the behaviors you observed, arrive at a total frequency of occurrence (sum the number of instances of the behavior over the thirty observation intervals). Divide this sum by the total number of intervals (in this case 30) and multiply the resulting number by 100. This will give you the percent occurrence of the observed behavior.

2. Compare the percentages across behaviors. What was the most frequent behavior? What was the least frequent behavior?

3. List the problems you encountered while making your observations (for example, participants moving too quickly, observations too difficult to make).

4. How could you have changed your observation to reduce the problems you encountered?

Doing an Ethnograpic Study

On a Saturday afternoon find a public place like a shopping mall, airport, zoo, or supermarket and do a brief (perhaps half-hour) ethnographic study. Make field notes of the behaviors you observe and the kinds of interactions your participants engage in. After making the initial observations, go back over your field notes and fill in any gaps that may exist. Then, analyze your qualitative data by looking for major themes, behaviors, and so on that emerge from your observations. Finally, do a content analysis of the more important behaviors that you have observed.

Doing a Sociometric Study

Find a small group (for example, children in a day care center, a committee, a small social group) and do a sociometric study. Devise a way to measure the interpersonal relationships among members of the group (for example, have members of the group select their first, second, and third choices for those with whom they would like to be friends). Represent your data on a chart like the one shown in Chapter 6 and then create a sociogram to graphically represent what you found.

Content Analysis

Another nonexperimental technique discussed in the text is content analysis. This exercise will give you practice using this technique. Choose one of the following hypotheses and test it using a content analysis:

1. Female characters in children's literature are more likely to be portrayed in a dependency role (that is, dependent on someone else for support, help, and so on) than are males.

2. The "good guys" in children's cartoon programming are more likely to be reinforced for using aggressive behavior than are the "bad guys."

To do this exercise you must obtain the necessary materials. For hypothesis 1 select at least five children's stories (you might include classic stories such as *Snow White* as well as some lesser known stories) and count the frequency with which females and males are portrayed in dependency roles. For hypothesis 2 watch five cartoon programs in which aggression occurs and record the number of times that aggression used by the hero is reinforced and the number of times aggression used by the villain is reinforced.

Before you begin your content analysis be sure to write out operational definitions for any variables being measured or used (for example, dependency, aggression, reinforced), and clearly indicate what your recording units and context units are (see Chapter 6 of your text for definitions of these terms).

Data Analysis

Once you have made your observations and collected your data, obtain an average for each category you included (male vs. female character or hero vs. villain), and answer the following questions:

1. Was the hypothesis supported by your observations?

2. If your hypothesis was not supported by your observations, could your content analysis be improved so that more accurate data could be collected? If so, what changes would you make?

3. List any difficulties you encountered in obtaining materials or collecting your data. What steps could you have taken to circumvent some of the problems that you encountered?

ANSWERS TO QUESTIONS AND EXERCISES

Multiple-Choice Questions

1. A	6. A	11. D	16. D
2. D	7. C	12. A	17. B
3. C	8. D	13. B	18. C
4. B	9. C	14. C	19. D
5. D	10. D	15. A	20. B

Fill-In Questions

1. make preliminary observations; conduct a literature review
2. behavior sequences
3. time sampling
4. participant observation, ethnography
5. describe a single case; compare cases
6. incomplete records; time-consuming process
7. recording units; context units
8. blind observers
9. qualitative
10. Ethnography
11. nonparticipant observation
12. gain access to the field setting
13. identify themes and hypotheses
14. Sociometry
15. sociogram
16. case study
17. existing records
18. content analysis
19. recording unit

CHAPTER 7

USING SURVEY RESEARCH

KEY QUESTIONS TO CONSIDER

- What are some of the applications of survey research?
- What are the steps involved in designing a questionnaire?
- How do open-ended and restricted questionnaire items differ? What are the advantages and disadvantages of each?
- How do you design effective rating scales?
- What general "rules" (for example, precision, biased questions) should you follow when writing questionnaire items? What could happen if these "rules" are violated?
- How do you arrange your items on a questionnaire?
- What are the different methods of administering a questionnaire? What are the advantages and disadvantages of each?
- What techniques are used to assess the reliability of a questionnaire?
- How can the reliability of a questionnaire be increased?
- What techniques are used to assess the validity of a questionnaire?
- What is a biased sample and why should you work hard to avoid it?
- What are the characteristics of the various sampling techniques used in survey research?
- How do you determine the size of the sample needed for a valid survey?

CHAPTER OUTLINE

Survey Research
Designing Your Questionnaire
    Selecting the Questionnaire Format
        Types of Questionnaire Items
        Rating Scales
        Writing Questionnaire Items
    Assembling the Questionnaire

REVIEW AND STUDY QUESTIONS

Key Term Definition

Define each of the following terms.

Open-ended item:

Restricted item:

Partially open-ended item:

Mail survey:

Nonresponse bias:

Telephone survey:

Interview:

Test–retest reliability:

Parallel-form reliability:

Split-half reliability:

Representative sample:

Biased sample:

Simple random sampling:

Stratified sampling:

Proportionate sampling:

Systematic sampling:

Cluster sampling:

Multistage sampling:

Sampling error:

Multiple-Choice Questions

Circle the alternative that best completes the stem of each question.

1. Surveys are used to
    a. establish causal relationships among variables.
    b. evaluate specific attitudes and behaviors.
    c. predict behavior.
    d. both b and c

2. It is important to properly design a questionnaire because
   a. an improperly designed questionnaire will preclude uncovering causal relationships among variables.
   b. an improperly designed questionnaire may yield data that are confusing and difficult to analyze.
   c. statistical techniques (for example, correlations) cannot be applied to items that are poorly worded.
   d. all of the above

3. On a questionnaire you include questions assessing each participant's age, sex, and income level. These variables are
   a. personality characteristics.
   b. criterion variables.
   c. demographics.
   d. independent variables.

4. The major advantage of an open-ended questionnaire item is that it
   a. provides participants with set response categories and thus limits the range of responses.
   b. can be used to help establish causal relationships among variables.
   c. yields information that is more complete than the information obtained with a more restricted item.
   d. none of the above

5. The multiple-choice items in this study guide would be classified as
   a. open-ended.
   b. restricted.
   c. partially restricted.
   d. partially open-ended.

6. The decision to label each point on a rating scale or only some of the points
   a. makes little difference.
   b. makes a big difference because labeling every point changes the underlying psychological dimension being measured.
   c. may make a big difference, especially when you are measuring a sensitive issue (for example, sexual behavior).
   d. is largely irrelevant because research shows that labeling each point is best.

7. "Do you think that AIDS is a punishment from God for vile homosexual behavior?" is an example of a questionnaire item that is
   a. vague.
   b. too simple.
   c. biased.
   d. too wordy.

8. According to the text, it is a good idea to put objectionable questions
   a. after less objectionable ones.
   b. first on your questionnaire to get them out of the way.
   c. in one place on your questionnaire, either before or after less objectionable ones.
   d. none of the above; objectionable items should not be included at all

9. A major problem with mail surveys is
   a. lack of continuity.
   b. nonresponse bias.
   c. that they are often confusing for participants to complete.
   d. all of the above

10. According to the text, when you conduct a telephone survey you should
    a. make sure your questions are worded clearly.
    b. limit the number of alternatives on restricted items.
    c. take extra care when asking a question that has ordered alternatives.
    d. do all of the above.

11. An advantage of conducting a survey on the Internet is
    a. you can reach many potential participants easily.
    b. data can be collected quickly and easily.
    c. you can be sure that your sample is more representative of the population than other questionnaire administration techniques.
    d. both a and b
    e. all of the above

12. According to your text, a disadvantage of conducting a survey on the Internet is
    a. surveys are too time consuming to run on the Internet.
    b. your sample of respondents may not be representative of the general population.
    c. you can only put short surveys on the Internet.
    d. you can only put noncontroversial questionnaires on the Internet.

13. The method of establishing the reliability of a questionnaire involving the administration of a questionnaire more than once is known as
    a. criterion-based reliability.
    b. test–retest reliability.
    c. internal consistency.
    d. split-half reliability.

14. Internal consistency involves establishing the reliability of a questionnaire by
    a. administering the same questionnaire repeatedly to the same participants.
    b. administering the same questionnaire repeatedly to different participants.
    c. inspecting the items on your questionnaire and making a decision whether the items are reliable.
    d. a single administration of your questionnaire.

15. When establishing _____, alternate forms of a questionnaire are administered to the same participants.
    a. parallel-form reliability
    b. split-half reliability
    c. internal consistency
    d. none of the above

16. According to the text, the best way to assess split-half reliability is to
    a. correlate items from the first half with items from the second half of your questionnaire.
    b. correlate odd-numbered items with even-numbered items.
    c. split your questionnaire up into at least four parts and correlate each part with all others.
    d. none of the above

17. According to the text, you can increase reliability by
    a. increasing the number of items on your questionnaire.
    b. scoring your questionnaire carefully.
    c. standardizing administration procedures.
    d. all of the above
    e. both a and c only

18. Which of the following would be a way to establish the validity of a questionnaire?
    a. Assessing content validity
    b. Assessing criterion-related validity
    c. Assessing test–retest validity
    d. all of the above
    e. both a and b only

19. A sample that includes participants whose characteristics closely match the characteristics of the population is
    a. valid.
    b. reliable.
    c. representative.
    d. responsive.

20. In a(n) _____ sample, every member of the population has an equal chance of appearing in your sample.
    a. random
    b. reliable
    c. unsystematic
    d. clustered

21. Stratified sampling is used to
    a. reduce nonresponse bias.
    b. ensure that members of different segments of a population are represented in your sample.
    c. reduce the randomness in sampling.
    d. none of the above

22. Sometimes stratified sampling does not solve the problem it is intended to solve and may even create more problems. If this is the case, then _____ is used.
    a. sampling with replacement
    b. cluster sampling
    c. proportionate sampling
    d. modified-stratified sampling

23. Two factors that enter into determining the number of participants needed to ensure a valid survey are
    a. population characteristics and sampling technique.
    b. administration technique and population characteristics.
    c. sampling technique and the amount of acceptable error.
    d. the amount of acceptable error and expected magnitude of proportions in the population.

24. The finite population correction is used when
    a. the population from which you sample is small.
    b. you want to correct for nonresponse bias.
    c. the population from which you sample is large.
    d. a minority group is overrepresented in your population.

Fill-In Questions

Fill in the blanks with the word or phrase that best completes each sentence.

1. Items on a questionnaire that measure the behavior you wish to predict are _____ _____.

2. A five-point rating scale used to measure the degree to which participants agree or disagree with a statement is a(n) _____.

3. A(n) _____ question elicits only the information in which you are interested.

4. According to the text, related items should be placed together on a questionnaire. This is known as _____.

5. One of the most effective methods for combatting nonresponse bias is to _____ _____.

6. A type of interview in which you ask specific questions in a specified order is a(n) _____ interview.

7. With _____ reliability you administer your questionnaire twice to the same participants; whereas with _____ you administer your questionnaire only once.

8. _____ reliability is a method of establishing reliability where you divide your questionnaire into two parts and correlate the items from the two parts.

9. If you were to establish validity by determining if the results of your questionnaire correlate well with another established questionnaire, you would be using _____ to establish validity.

10. According to the text, the *Literary Digest* poll failed because _____ _____.

11. Once a participant is chosen for your sample, he or she cannot be chosen again. This sampling technique is known as _____.

12. A variant of simple random sampling that can be used when conducting a telephone survey is _____.

13. To combat the problem of minority groups being overrepresented in a stratified sampling scheme, you can use _____.

14. _____ is a sampling technique that involves selecting every *k*th participant after a random start.

15. A good sampling technique to use when you have several large naturally occurring groups (for example, school districts) that could be included in your sample is _____ _____.

16. A(n) _____ includes enough participants to ensure a valid survey, and no more.

17. Because of _____, you can never be sure that the characteristics of your sample exactly match those of the population.

Essay Questions

1. Discuss the factors you must consider when writing questionnaire items. How does each factor affect the nature of the information acquired?

2. Discuss the factors that must be considered when assembling a questionnaire.

3. List and discuss the methods you can use to fight nonresponse bias in a mail survey.

4. Although a telephone survey may be more desirable in some ways than a mail survey, there are drawbacks. List and discuss two factors that must be considered when deciding to use a telephone survey.

5. Describe and discuss the ways that you could assess the reliability and validity of a questionnaire. What could you do to increase reliability?

6. Shere Hite mailed 100,000 questionnaires to several women's groups (for example, feminist organizations, church women's organizations) in several states (*Time,* October 12, 1987). After obtaining an initial response rate of about 1,500, she attempted to acquire other participants to fill in demographic gaps. In response to criticism that her sample was not representative, Hite said, "It's 4,500 people. That's enough for me" (*Time,* October 12, 1987, p. 71).

   Evaluate Hite's claim that 4,500 respondents is "good enough." Based on the discussion of the problem of biased samples in the text, do you agree or disagree with this statement? Justify your agreement or disagreement.

EXERCISING YOUR KNOWLEDGE

Designing a Questionnaire

This exercise will give you some experience in writing and administering a questionnaire. Select a topic as the focus of a brief questionnaire. Your topic should be some nonsensitive issue (for example, a campus-related issue; avoid sensitive topics such as sexuality or criminal behavior) and have your topic approved by your instructor. Then develop several questions (15 at the most) designed to assess attitudes and/or behavior relative to your topic. Include a couple of demographic items (age, sex, marital status, for example) on your questionnaire.

Your questionnaire should include at least one of each type of item discussed in Chapter 7 of your text (open-ended, restricted, partially open-ended, and rating scale). Assemble your items into a brief questionnaire according to the advice given in Chapter 7 and administer it to between five and ten participants. (You might also want to prepare a brief informed consent form for your participants to sign.)

Data Analysis

When you have collected your data, perform the following simple data analyses:

1. Summarize by participant the responses to each item on a data-coding sheet.

2. Check to see if your items produced at least some response variability. You do not want an item to elicit the same response from everyone!

3. Are there some items that appear to be "good" or "bad" items? If so, what makes them good or bad?

4. Think about how you would go about analyzing your data to establish relationships between your demographic items and your attitude or behavior items (you may need to consult an introductory-level statistics book to answer this question). Could your items have been worded or presented differently so as to yield data that would be easier to analyze?

5. Identify any questions you think should be revised, and suggest changes to make them better.

Popular Questionnaires

Publications such as *Psychology Today, Redbook,* and so on sometimes have short questionnaires designed to help readers find out about themselves. Go to the library, find such a questionnaire in a magazine, and do the following:

1. Identify the topic on which the questionnaire focused.

2. Evaluate each question according to the discussion in Chapter 7. For example, how well were the questions worded? Did the questions have words that are difficult to understand? If restricted items were used, evaluate them for precision and comprehensiveness of alternatives. Rewrite any questions you think could be improved.

3. Note the format of the questionnaire. Was it easy to complete? Did it have continuity? Suggest changes you would make to improve the questionnaire.

4. Finally, indicate whether or not you think such "self-disclosure" questionnaires are a good idea. Why or why not?

Participating in an Internet Survey

Find a survey on the Internet that interests you and participate in it. The easiest way to find on-line surveys is to do a net search using Yahoo. Click on **science,** then **psychology,** and finally **tests and experiments.** You will find several examples of surveys being conducted on the Internet. As you are participating, note down the following:

1. Was the survey instrument on-line or did you have to give your e-mail address to have one sent to you?

2. How many questions were on the questionnaire?

3. How long did it take to complete the questionnaire?

4. What format(s) was used for the questions?

5. Was the questionnaire easy to complete?

6. Did you detect any problems or flaws with the questionnaire or the manner in which it was administered?

7. Were you given the option of obtaining a copy of the results when the survey was finished? (If so, be sure to send for them!)

Learning How to Post a Survey on the Internet

For this exercise you will need to find the on-line tutorial on how to post surveys on the Internet at the following address: <http://salmon.psy.plym.ac.uk/mscprm/forms.htm>. Read through the documentation and then try your hand at putting a short questionnaire on the Internet.

ANSWERS TO QUESTIONS

Multiple-Choice Questions

1. D	9. B	17. D
2. B	10. D	18. E
3. C	11. D	19. C
4. C	12. B	20. A
5. B	13. B	21. B
6. A	14. D	22. C
7. C	15. A	23. D
8. A	16. B	24. A

Fill-In Questions

1. criterion variables
2. Likert scale
3. precise
4. continuity
5. send follow-up letters
6. structured
7. test–retest; internal consistency
8. Split-half
9. criterion-related validity
10. the sample was biased
11. sampling without replacement
12. random digit dialing
13. proportionate sampling
14. Systematic sampling
15. cluster sampling
16. economic sample
17. sampling error

CHAPTER 8

USING BETWEEN-SUBJECTS AND WITHIN-SUBJECTS EXPERIMENTAL DESIGNS

KEY QUESTIONS TO CONSIDER

- How do between-subjects, within-subjects, and single-subject experiments differ?
- How might error variance in a between-subjects design affect your results and what steps can be taken to handle it?
- How are statistics used to test the reliability of data from a between-subjects experiment?
- How does a randomized group experiment work? What are some of its advantages and disadvantages?
- When would you use a matched-groups design?
- How does a matched-pairs design differ from a matched-groups design?
- What are some of the advantages and disadvantages of the matching strategy?
- What are the advantages and disadvantages of within-subjects designs?
- How do carryover effects influence interpretation of the results from a within-subjects experiment?
- Under what conditions will counterbalancing be effective or ineffective in dealing with carryover effects?
- When do you use a Latin square design?
- What steps can you take to handle carryover effects?
- Do between-subjects and within-subjects designs applied to the same variables always produce the same functional relationships?
- When should you consider using a within-subjects design over a between-subjects design?
- When should you consider using a matched groups design rather than a within-subjects design?
- How do single-factor and multiple-factor designs differ and why would you use a multiple-factor design?
- What is a main effect and how does it differ from an interaction?
- How does a confounding variable affect the validity of your results and how can confounding be eliminated?

CHAPTER OUTLINE

Types of Experimental Design
The Problem of Error Variance in Between-Subjects and Within-Subjects Designs
    Sources of Error Variance
    Handling Error Variance
        Reducing Error Variance
        Increasing the Effectiveness of Your Independent Variable
        Randomizing Error Variance Across Groups
        Statistical Analysis
Between-Subjects Designs
    The Single-Factor Randomized Groups Designs
        The Randomized Two-Group Design
        The Randomized Multigroup Design
    Matched Groups Designs
        Logic of the Matched Groups Design
        Advantages and Disadvantages of the Matched Groups Design
        The Matched Pairs Design
        Matched Multigroup Designs
Within-Subjects Designs
    Advantages of the Within-Subjects Design
    Disadvantages of the Within-Subjects Design
    Sources of Carryover
    Dealing With Carryover Effects
        Counterbalancing
        Taking Steps to Minimize Carryover
        Making Treatment Order an Independent Variable
    When to Use a Within-Subjects Design
        Subject Variables Correlated With the Dependent Variable
        Economizing on Subjects
        Assessing the Effects of Increasing Exposure on Behavior
    Within-Subjects Versus Matched Groups Designs
    Types of Within-Subjects Designs
        The Single-Factor Two-Level Design
        Single-Factor Multilevel Designs
Designs With Two or More Independent Variables
    Factorial Designs
        Main Effects
        Interactions
        Factorial Within-Subjects Designs
        Higher-Order Factorial Designs
    Other Group-Based Designs

Designs With Two or More Dependent Variables
Confounding and Experimental Design
Summary
Key Terms

REVIEW AND STUDY QUESTIONS

Key Term Definition

Define each of the following terms.

  Between-subjects design:

  Within-subject design:

  Single-subject design:

  Error variance:

  Randomized two-group design:

  Parametric design:

  Nonparametric design:

  Multiple control group design:

  Matched groups design:

  Matched pairs design:

  Carryover effects:

  Counterbalancing:

  Latin square design:

  Factorial design:

  Main effect:

Interaction:

Higher order factorial designs:

Multiple-Choice Questions

Circle the alternative that best completes the stem of each question.

1. In a between-subjects design
   a. all subjects receive every level of the independent variable.
   b. one or a few subjects are studied extensively at all levels of the independent variable.
   c. each subject receives only one level of the independent variable.
   d. data are analyzed by plotting the performances of single subjects.

2. Within-subjects designs differ from between-subjects designs in that
   a. only one group of subjects is used.
   b. only one subject participates at each level of the independent variable.
   c. only variables "within" the subject are examined, such as heart rate.
   d. all of the above are true.

3. Unwanted variations in environmental conditions and subject characteristics that affect your dependent variable
   a. do not affect the results of between-subjects designs.
   b. constitute the independent variable.
   c. produce error variance.
   d. can be completely eliminated through proper experimental design.

4. Error variance comes from
   a. differences between subjects in their characteristics.
   b. moment-to-moment changes in subject characteristics.
   c. environmental conditions that are not absolutely constant.
   d. all of the above

5. To deal with the effects of error variance in a between-subjects design, you can
   a. attempt to hold extraneous variables constant.
   b. increase the effectiveness of your independent variable.
   c. randomize error variance across groups.
   d. do any of the above.

6. You assess the reliability of effects in between-subjects designs by
   a. using inferential statistics.
   b. comparing a single subject's performance across repeated exposures to the same level of the independent variable.
   c. checking whether the samples adequately represent the population.
   d. all of the above

7. A limitation of the randomized two-group design is that you
   a. cannot determine whether the independent variable has a reliable effect.
   b. must use extremely large groups of subjects to detect an effect of your independent variable.
   c. do not learn much about the function relating the independent and dependent variables.
   d. cannot apply parametric inferential statistics to the data.

8. Your between-subjects design manipulates a single variable across several quantitative levels. It would be described as a _____ design.
   a. two-group
   b. single-factor parametric
   c. single-factor nonparametric
   d. factorial

9. The multiple control group design is used when
   a. a single control group is not adequate to rule out alternative explanations for your results.
   b. the level of a drug is the independent variable.
   c. a placebo control group would not be a good idea.
   d. multiple *t* tests will be used to analyze the data.

10. An advantage of using matching rather than simple random assignment to form your groups is that
    a. matching reduces error due to subject differences.
    b. matching is easier to do than randomization.
    c. matching eliminates any possible correlation between the scores in the two treatments.
    d. all of the above are advantages.

11. A disadvantage of matched groups design is that
    a. you must take the extra step of matching subjects prior to assigning them to groups.
    b. matching will improve the sensitivity of the experiment only if the matched characteristic has a relatively large effect on the dependent variable.
    c. you must be sure that the instrument you use to determine the match is valid and reliable.
    d. all of the above are disadvantages.

12. Unlike two-group designs, multigroup parametric designs allow you to
    a. determine whether an independent variable has an effect on a dependent variable.
    b. examine the data for trend.
    c. control extraneous variables.
    d. all of the above

13. In a within-subjects experiment, you
    a. randomly assign subjects to different treatment groups.
    b. examine the individual performance of a single subject across several treatments.
    c. expose a single group of subjects to all the treatments.
    d. ask participants to report what is going on "within" their minds.

14. An advantage of the within-subjects design is that it
    a. tends to be more powerful than the equivalent between-subjects design.
    b. eliminates the problem of carryover effects.
    c. is less susceptible to confounding than other designs.
    d. does all of the above.

15. When using a within-subjects design (as opposed to a between-subjects design), you can often
    a. make do with fewer subjects.
    b. save on materials and money.
    c. reduce the time required to debrief participants.
    d. do all of the above.

16. A disadvantage to using a within-subjects design (as opposed to a between-subjects design) is that
    a. each subject must spend more time in the experiment.
    b. carryover effects must be controlled for.
    c. participant attrition may be a more serious problem.
    d. all the above are possible disadvantages.

17. If exposing subjects to a treatment alters the subjects' responses to a subsequent treatment, the data suffer from
    a. response differential.
    b. carryover.
    c. external validity.
    d. internal validity.

18. If you are told that break-ins are occurring in your neighborhood during the night, house noises you used to ignore may now awaken you. This phenomenon is called
    a. adaptation.
    b. habituation.
    c. sensitization.
    d. contrast.

19. A completely counterbalanced design deals with order effects by
    a. averaging them out across treatments.
    b. eliminating them.
    c. including only some of the possible treatment orders, with the restriction that each treatment appear in each position an equal number of times.
    d. reducing them to tolerable levels through instructions to the participants.

20. If you make the number of treatment orders in your design equal to the number of treatments, you can use a _____ design to keep each treatment appearing an equal number of times at each ordinal position.
    a. completely counterbalanced
    b. nested
    c. mixed
    d. Latin square

21. Counterbalancing can be counted on to control order effects only if
    a. the order effects induced by different orders are of different magnitudes.
    b. the order effects induced by different orders are of the same approximate magnitude.
    c. order effects are vanishingly small compared to the treatment effects.
    d. adaptation or habituation is responsible for the order effects.

22. The most serious asymmetry in carryover effects occurs when a treatment produces
    a. habituation.
    b. fatigue.
    c. sensitization.
    d. irreversible changes.

23. Making treatment order an independent variable enables you to
    a. eliminate carryover effects.
    b. reduce the effects of sensitization and fatigue.
    c. measure the size of any carryover effect.
    d. decrease the number of subjects required by your design.

24. To deal with carryover effects, you can
    a. counterbalance the order of treatments.
    b. make treatment order an independent variable.
    c. take steps to reduce carryover.
    d. all of the above

25. A strong carryover effect can be a problem with within-subjects designs. If you wish to retain some of the advantage of the within-subject design but must avoid carryover, you should substitute a _____ design.
    a. factorial between-subjects design.
    b. matched groups design.
    c. randomized groups design.
    d. correlational design.

26. An experiment exposes all participants to five advertising styles (in counterbalanced order) and assesses desire for the product following each exposure. The experiment follows a _____ within-subjects design.
    a. single-factor, multilevel
    b. five-factor factorial
    c. nested
    d. multivariate

27. In a factorial design, if the effect of Variable A (on the dependent measure) changes with the level of Variable B, then
    a. the results are hopelessly confounded.
    b. an interaction is present.
    c. there are no main effects of the two independent variables.
    d. the dependent variable is insensitive.

28. A serious problem with using factorial designs having a large number of factors is that
    a. they require a large number of subjects.
    b. the complex interactions that may emerge are difficult to interpret.
    c. there are no statistical analyses available for such designs.
    d. both a and b

29. You plan to conduct a factorial experiment in which there are three levels of Factor A and four levels of Factor B. You intend to use 10 subjects per group. How many subjects will you need for the experiment?
    a. 10
    b. 70
    c. 120
    d. 240

30. A multivariate design always includes
    a. several levels of the independent variable.
    b. two or more dependent variables.
    c. two or more independent variables.
    d. all of the above

31. A good reason to use a multivariate design is to
    a. construct a composite dependent variable that may be more strongly related to your independent variable than any single dependent variable is.
    b. examine several dependent variables simultaneously to determine which is the most sensitive to the independent variable.
    c. get a better understanding of what is going on "beneath the surface," as inferred from your dependent variables.
    d. all of the above

Fill-In Questions

Fill in the blanks with the word or phrase that best completes each sentence.

1. The data from a between-subjects experiment must be submitted to a(n) _____ _____ in order to determine whether any group differences in performance are reliable.

2. If a difference between group means is found to be statistically significant, you can conclude that the results are probably _____.

3. If all subjects in an experiment are exposed to all of the levels of the independent variable, and the results are then statistically averaged over subjects, the experiment follows a(n) _____ design.

4. The variation in scores across subjects that is produced by extraneous variables in an experiment is called _____ variance.

5. Assigning participants to groups by drawing names out of a hat would be a crude example of the technique of _____.

6. In the _____ design, subjects are assigned at random to one or the other of two groups.

7. If the levels of the independent variable represent quantitative (as opposed to qualitative) differences, a design is described as _____.

8. In a(n) _____ design, there is one group for every combination of levels of the independent variables.

9. Where the expectations of subjects concerning the effect of a treatment (such as a drug) may affect the dependent variable, you would want to include a(n) _____ group in the design.

10. If subjects are first matched into pairs on some variable or variables, and then each pair is randomly split between two groups, the experiment follows a _____ design.

11. _____ occur when a previous treatment alters the behavior observed in a subsequent treatment.

12. Changes in performance that occur because subjects can compare what happens in one treatment to what happens in another are due to _____.

13. _____ involves assigning the various treatments of an experiment in a different order for different subjects.

14. If every possible order of treatments is represented exactly once, your design is said to be _____ counterbalanced.

15. If only some of the possible treatment orders are included in a design, it is said to be _____ counterbalanced.

16. You can use a Latin square to determine the order of treatments in your design if you choose to make the number of treatment orders equal to the number of _____.

17. If carryover from Treatment A to Treatment B is greater than carryover from Treatment B to Treatment A, your design suffers from the problem of _____ carryover effects.

18. When changes in the level of the dependent variable are caused by a given treatment and these changes cannot be undone by subsequent changes, the changes are said to be _____.

19. The main advantage of making order of treatments an independent variable is that you can assess the size of any _____.

20. You should strongly consider using a within-subjects design when _____ differences contribute heavily to variation in the dependent variable.

21. The column sums and row sums in the results of a factorial experiment represent the _____ of the experiment.

22. Two lines on a graph represent the effect of Variable A on reaction time at two levels of Variable B. If the lines are _____, then an interaction is *not* present.

23. _____ designs simultaneously assess the effects of an independent variable on two or more dependent variables.

24. Confounding variables affect the _____ of a design.

Essay Questions

1. Briefly describe the between-subjects, within-subjects, and single-subject approaches to experimental design.

2. Discuss how inferential statistics assess the reliability of a difference between the group mean in a randomized two-groups experiment.

3. Describe what steps you would take to deal with the problem of error variance in a between-subjects design.

4. Why is it preferable to use a multigroup design rather than several two-group designs?

5. Describe the logic behind the matched groups design and indicate when such a design would be used.

6. List and describe the major advantages and disadvantages of the within-subjects design.

7. List and describe the six sources of carryover effects.

8. What techniques are available to handle carryover effects? Under what conditions will they work the best or not work well?

9. Identify several possible sources of confounding in between-subjects designs and describe how to avoid them.

EXERCISING YOUR KNOWLEDGE

Conducting a Matched Pairs Experiment

Imagine you are about to conduct an experiment investigating reaction times as a function of stimulus complexity. You are concerned that your participants may show great differences in reaction times even when the participants are treated identically. These differences may obscure any effect of stimulus complexity. You have reason to believe that participants of the same sex and approximate age will be more similar to one another than randomly selected participants, so you decide to match on these two variables.

Following is a list of participants, together with their sexes and ages. Form matched pairs of participants based on these variables. Then use the table of random numbers found in the Appendix of your text to assign the first member of each pair to either Group A or Group B. Assign the remaining member of each pair to the opposite group. Show each step of your work (matching and group assignment).

Participant	Sex	Age	Participant	Sex	Age
1	Male	21	11	Female	20
2	Male	19	12	Male	42
3	Female	31	13	Female	23
4	Female	25	14	Female	18
5	Male	34	15	Male	24
6	Female	22	16	Female	46
7	Male	25	17	Male	18
8	Female	35	18	Male	29
9	Male	27	19	Female	24
10	Male	22	20	Female	32

Interpreting Data From Factorial Designs

The following statistics resulted from analysis of data from a 2 × 2 factorial experiment. Calculate the row and column sums. Then plot these sums on graph paper and connect the points to show the effects of the independent variables. What can you say about the effect of word type? About the effect of instruction? Did the two independent variables interact? Explain why you drew these conclusions.

Level of Instruction	Level of Word Type		Column Sums
	High Imagery	Low Imagery	
Imagery	10.57	5.86	
Rehearsal	8.57	2.29	
Row Sums			

Results of Analysis of Variance

$$\text{Word Type:} \quad F(1, 24) = 41.08, p < .01$$
$$\text{Instruction:} \quad F(1, 24) = 10.54, p < .01$$
$$WT \times I \text{ Interaction:} \quad F(1, 24) = 0.84, \text{ns}$$

Seek-and-Destroy Mission

Identify the sources of confounding in the following experiment. Then describe how you would change the design to eliminate them.

The experiment was designed to evaluate the effect of "subliminal perception" on thirst. The participants (college sophomores) were randomly assigned to two groups. One group watched a movie (*Return of the Pink Panther*) that did not contain subliminal messages. The other group watched a movie (*The Desert Fox*) in which the message "Have a cool drink!" was repeatedly flashed on the screen so quickly that it was not consciously noticeable. Because of time limitations, the first group watched the movie at 8:30 A.M., the second at 11:30 A.M. The dependent measure was the amount of icewater consumed by the participants as they watched the movie. Results showed that the subliminal messages apparently worked: The second group drank significantly more icewater than the first.

Counterbalancing

You want to conduct an experiment investigating the detection rate for stray aircraft on a radar screen as a function of the number of aircraft already present. (The radar screen will be simulated by computer.) There will be four levels of aircraft present (4, 8, 16, and 32), and you suspect that participants will differ widely in their basic abilities to detect stimuli in the complex environment represented by the display. Show how you would arrange the order of treatments for each of 12 participants. How many participants would be required for an equivalent between-subjects design? In addition to the economy of participants, why would the within-subjects design be preferable?

Conducting a Within-Subjects Experiment

Draw an inverted "T" on a sheet of typing paper, using a ruler. The horizontal line should be drawn four inches above and parallel to the bottom edge of the paper. It should be four inches long and centered between the left and right edges. The vertical line should begin at the center of the horizontal line and should extend six inches toward the top, perpendicular to the horizontal line.

Now show the figure to 10 of your friends, relatives, or other suitable victims. Each person should view two of the sheets, one presented with the "T" inverted, and one presented with the "T" lying on its side, with the stem pointing toward the right. Half of your participants should see the inverted "T" first, half the sideways "T" first. Assign the order of presentation at random.

For each figure, have participants mark the stem of the "T" at the position where the stem length appears equal to the length of the crossbar.

Measure the stem lengths marked by the participants, and record them separately for vertical and horizontal "T"s. Compute the mean and standard deviation for each "T" position. Use the t test for correlated samples to assess the reliability of any difference. (Don't forget to use the appropriate calculation for degrees of freedom!) Determine whether the difference in treatment means was statistically significant. What is your conclusion?

ANSWERS TO QUESTIONS AND EXERCISES

Multiple-Choice Questions

1.	C	12.	B	23.	C
2.	A	13.	C	24.	D
3.	C	14.	A	25.	B
4.	D	15.	D	26.	A
5.	D	16.	D	27.	B
6.	A	17.	B	28.	D
7.	C	18.	C	29.	C
8.	B	19.	A	30.	B
9.	A	20.	D	31.	D
10.	A	21.	B		
11.	D	22.	D		

Fill-In Questions

1. statistical analysis
2. reliable
3. within-subjects
4. error

5. random assignment
6. randomized two-group
7. parametric
8. factorial
9. placebo control
10. matched pairs
11. Carryover effects
12. contrast
13. Counterbalancing
14. completely
15. partially
16. treatments
17. differential
18. irreversible
19. carryover effects
20. subject
21. main effects
22. parallel
23. Multivariate
24. internal validity

Exercising Your Knowledge

Conducting a Matched Pairs Experiment

One way to match partcipants would be to begin by separating the males and females. Then rank-order the participants in each group according to age. In the example you would get the following:

Males: 18, 19, 21, 22, 24, 25, 27, 29, 34, 42
Females: 18, 20, 22, 23, 24, 25, 31, 32, 35, 46

Now assign one member of each pair at random to Group A or Group B. You could begin at an arbitrary location within the table of random numbers. If the first number is odd, then place the first male on the rank-ordered list in Group A; otherwise, place him in Group B. Then assign the second male to the opposite group. Taking the next two males on the list, follow the same procedure, and continue this way until all participants (male and female) have been assigned to groups. The result might look like this:

Participant	Random No.	Group	Participant	Group
M 18	3	A	M 19	B
M 21	5	A	M 22	B
M 24	8	B	M 25	A
M 27	1	A	M 29	B
M 34	4	B	M 42	A

Participant	Random No.	Group	Participant	Group
F 18	2	B	F 20	A
F 22	6	B	F 23	A
F 24	7	A	F 25	B
F 31	9	A	F 32	B
F 35	0	B	F 46	A

Interpreting Data From Factorial Designs

Summing the columns gives 19.14 for the high-imagery words and 8.15 for the low-imagery words. The difference between these is statistically significant (main effect of word type). Summing the rows gives 16.43 for the imagery instruction, 10.86 for the rehearsal instruction. This effect is also statistically significant (main effect of instruction). Plotting group means reveals approximately parallel lines, and the interaction term, predictably, is not significant. Conclusion: High-imagery words are recalled better than low-imagery words, regardless of instructions, and instructions to use imagery produce better recall than do instructions to rehearse, regardless of whether the words are high imagery or low imagery.

Seek-and-Destroy Mission

Although participants are randomly assigned to conditions (eliminating bias in participant assignment), differences in the treatment of the two groups lead to confounding. The two groups saw different movies, and *The Desert Fox* movie could have produced more thirst (by showing desert scenes) than the *Return of the Pink Panther* movie. Also, the two groups were tested at different times of day. Participants may have been thirstier at 11:30 A.M. than at 8:30 A.M. The confounding could be eliminated by showing both groups the same movie (with or without subliminal messages) and counterbalancing the times at which the movie was shown to the two groups (half of each group seeing it at 8:30, half at 11:30).

CHAPTER 9

USING SPECIALIZED RESEARCH DESIGNS

KEY QUESTIONS TO CONSIDER

- What is a mixed design and when is it used?
- What is a nested design and when is it used?
- What are the various types of nesting that can be done? Why might you use each?
- When would you consider using a design that combines experimental and correlational components?
- What is the definition of a quasi-independent variable?
- What are the advantages and disadvantages of including a quasi-independent variable in your experimental design?
- What are the characteristics of the time series designs and equivalent time samples design?
- What are the advantages and disadvantages of quasi-experimental designs?
- How are problems of internal validity addressed in a quasi-experimental design?
- What is the nonequivalent control group design? What are its strengths and weaknesses?
- What are the defining characteristics of the pretest–posttest design and what are some of the design's advantages and disadvantages?
- What is a Solomon four-group design and why would you consider using it?
- What are the defining qualities of the cross-sectional developmental design?
- What are the advantages and disadvantages of the cross-sectional design?
- What is a longitudinal developmental design?
- What are the advantages and disadvantages of the longitudinal design?
- What are the defining characteristics of the cohort-sequential developmental design?
- What are the advantages and disadvantages of the cohort-sequential design?

CHAPTER OUTLINE

Combining Between-Subjects and Within-Subjects Designs
    The Mixed Design

REVIEW AND STUDY QUESTIONS

Key Term Definition

Define each of the following terms.

Mixed design:

Nested design:

Covariate:

Quasi-independent variable:

Quasi-experimental design:

Time series design:

Interrupted time series design:

Equivalent time samples design:

Nonequivalent control group design:

Pretest–posttest design:

Solomon four-group design:

Cross-sectional design:

Longitudinal design:

Cohort-sequential design:

Multiple-Choice Questions

Circle the alternative that best completes the stem of each question.

1. A mixed design includes
   a. both a single factor and a parametric factor.
   b. both within-subjects and between-subjects factors.
   c. both experimental and correlational factors.
   d. multiple independent and dependent variables.

2. In an experiment on learning you have three levels of word list difficulty. Under each level of difficulty you have two different lists of words. The design being used here is a
   a. nested design.
   b. quasi-experimental design.
   c. mixed design.
   d. design combining correlational and experimental components.

3. A design that combines correlational and experimental components is used when
   a. you must economize on research participants.
   b. a within-subjects design becomes impractical.
   c. you want to statistically control the effects of a variable on which participants vary.
   d. both a and b
   e. none of the above

4. A correlational variable that resembles an independent variable is known as a(n)
   a. quasi-independent variable.
   b. quasi-experimental variable.
   c. covariate.
   d. pseudo-experimental variable.

5. An advantage of including a quasi-independent variable in an experiment is that the quasi-independent variable
   a. allows you to assess the generality of your findings across the levels of the quasi-independent variable.
   b. makes it more difficult to misinterpret your results.
   c. allows you to infer a causal relationship between your quasi-independent variable and dependent variable.
   d. totally eliminates confounding variables from your design.

6. According to your text, the main disadvantage of including a quasi-independent variable in an experiment is that
   a. it adds complexity to an experiment.
   b. results are often misinterpreted.
   c. it is difficult to quantify quasi-independent variables.
   d. adding a quasi-independent variable adds potential confounding variables to an experiment.

7. In a _____ you make observations prior to and immediately after introducing your independent variable.
   a. nonequivalent time samples design
   b. time series design
   c. pretest–posttest design
   d. none of the above

8. In the interrupted time series design, the independent variable is
   a. a true independent variable created by the experimenter.
   b. limited to participant variables such as age and sex.
   c. statistically controlled to remove its effects on the dependent variable.
   d. often a naturally occurring event and therefore not a true independent variable.

9. A quasi-experimental design in which the independent variable is presented repeatedly is the
   a. equivalent control groups design.
   b. multiple time series design.
   c. equivalent time samples design.
   d. nonequivalent control group design.

10. According to your text, an advantage of quasi-experimental designs is that
    a. they allow you to evaluate the impact of a quasi-independent variable under naturally occurring conditions.
    b. you can statistically control extraneous variables to clarify the relationship between a true independent variable and the dependent variable.
    c. you have a high degree of control over the variables that control behavior.
    d. both a and b
    e. all of the above

11. A drawback of quasi-experimental research is that
    a. you can never establish causal relationships.
    b. when you are using naturally occurring events, you have little or no control over when the event will occur.
    c. you cannot control participant characteristics such as age and gender.
    d. both a and c
    e. all of the above

12. In a nonequivalent control group design,
    a. a covariate is included.
    b. a control group is included that is not exposed to the treatment to which the experimental group is exposed.
    c. only one observation is made before introducing the independent variable.
    d. none of the above

13. Pretest–posttest designs are used to
    a. test a participant's ability to perform on multiple tests.
    b. make sure a research procedure works (by pretesting it) before actually conducting a study.
    c. evaluate performance only in classroom situations.
    d. evaluate the effects of some change in the environment on subsequent performance.

14. According to your text, the pretest–posttest design differs from quasi-experimental designs in that
    a. quasi-experimental designs are more powerful than pretest–posttest designs.
    b. it is not possible to establish causal relationships in a pretest–posttest design, whereas it is possible in a quasi-experimental design.
    c. the pretest–posttest design is a true experimental design resembling a within-subjects design.
    d. you have less control over extraneous variables with the pretest–posttest design than with the quasi-experimental design.

15. A problem you need to be concerned with specifically when using a pretest–posttest design (as opposed to other designs) is
    a. the possible effects of the pretest itself on subsequent performance.
    b. the validity of the dependent variable.
    c. the effect of the posttest on subsequent performance.
    d. the range of the independent variable.

16. A pretest–posttest design that allows you to test for possible sensitizing effects of a pretest is the
    a. nonequivalent control group design.
    b. Solomon four-group design.
    c. Latin square design.
    d. multiple pretest design.

17. A developmental design that involves measuring different-aged participants at about the same time is the _____ design.
    a. cross-sectional
    b. longitudinal
    c. cohort-generational
    d. cohort-sequential

18. In a cross-sectional design testing memory over the lifespan, _____ may preclude drawing clear conclusions based on the observations made.
    a. subject mortality
    b. a cross-generation problem
    c. a generation effect
    d. a multiple testing effect

19. A developmental design that involves measuring the same participants over some period of time is the _____ design.
    a. cross-sectional
    b. quasi-developmental
    c. experimental-developmental
    d. longitudinal

20. Cross-generation effects, subject mortality, and multiple testing effects are problems for which developmental design?
    a. The cross-sectional design
    b. The longitudinal design
    c. The cohort-sequential design
    d. all of the above

21. The cohort-sequential design allows you to
    a. test for the presence of generation effects.
    b. eliminate generation effects.
    c. reduce multiple testing effects.
    d. draw causal inferences from a developmental design.

Fill-In Questions

1. Between-subjects and within-subjects components are both included in a(n) _____ design.

2. If you need to test participants in large groups, a(n) _____ design can be useful.

3. A correlational variable (for example, gender) you include in an experiment to statistically control is known as a(n)_____.

4. A(n) _____ is a correlational variable that resembles a true independent variable in an experiment.

5. The potential for frequently misinterpreting results is a problem associated with _____.

6. In a _____ design you make several observations before and after introducing an independent variable.

7. A nonexperimental design in which you chart behavior as a function of a naturally occurring event is the _____ design.

8. In the _____ design, the independent variable is administered repeatedly.

9. In the _____ design one group of participants is exposed to your independent variable and another, different group, is not.

10. Unlike quasi-experimental designs like the time series design, the pretest–posttest design is _____.

11. The _____ design allows you to test for pretest sensitization effects.

12. In a developmental design the age of a participant is always considered to be a(n) _____.

13. In the _____ design you select participants from two or more age groups and study them over a short period of time.

14. _____, which may affect the results of a cross-sectional study, may occur when participants of widely differing ages are used.

15. In a _____ design, a group of subjects is followed over some period of time and measured repeatedly.

16. Because of _____ the results from a longitudinal study may not generalize very well.

17. Two disadvantages of the longitudinal developmental design are _____ and _____.

18. The _____ design allows you to test for the presence of generation effects.

19. The cohort-sequential design includes both a(n) _____ component and a(n) _____ component.

Essay Questions

1. Outline the general strategy behind the mixed design and give a research example in which you would use the design.

2. Describe the various ways that a nested design can be carried out. Give examples of when nesting would be beneficial.

3. Discuss the strengths and weaknesses of quasi-experimental research. What methods can be used to reduce some of the validity problems inherent in this type of research?

4. Describe each of the quasi-experimental designs discussed in the text and indicate when each design might be used.

5. Describe the basic strategy involved in the pretest–posttest design. What problems arise when this design is used?

6. Describe how the Solomon four-group design can be used to test for some of the problems inherent in the pretest–posttest design.

7. Compare and contrast the three developmental designs. Include in your discussion the advantages and disadvantages of each.

8. How do the problems of generation effects, subject mortality, and multiple observation effects affect the results from a longitudinal design? What, if anything, can be done about them?

EXERCISING YOUR KNOWLEDGE

Using Mixed Designs

Go to the library and find a research study that employed a mixed design. Identify the between-subjects and within-subjects variables. Why do you think that the researcher(s) used a mixed design? Could the same experiment have been run as a straight between-subjects or within-subjects experiment? Why or why not? How were the data analyzed and reported? Finally, design your own mixed experiment to test a hypothesis related to the topic of the paper you read.

Designing a Quasi-Experimental Study

Design a quasi-experimental study to test the hypothesis that there are more suicides reported after a well-publicized suicide is reported in the press. Identify the source of your observations prior to the naturally occurring event and after. How would you conduct your study and what problems might you encounter?

Identifying and Analyzing Developmental Designs

Once again, go to the library and find an example of a cross-sectional, longitudinal, and cohort-sequential design. Make special note of how the study was carried out. What did the researchers do, if anything, to address the problems inherent in developmental designs (for example, generation effects, cross-generation effects, subject mortality, multiple observations)? Was the author careful when interpreting the relationship between age and the dependent variable?

ANSWERS TO QUESTIONS AND EXERCISES

Multiple-Choice Questions

1.	B	12.	B
2.	A	13.	D
3.	C	14.	C
4.	A	15.	A
5.	A	16.	B
6.	B	17.	A
7.	B	18.	C
8.	D	19.	D
9.	C	20.	B
10.	A	21.	A
11.	B		

Fill-In Questions

1. mixed
2. nested
3. covariate
4. quasi-independent variable
5. quasi-experimental research
6. time series
7. interrupted time series
8. equivalent time samples
9. nonequivalent control group
10. a true experimental design
11. Solomon four-group
12. correlational variable
13. cross-sectional
14. Generation effects
15. longitudinal
16. cross-generation effects
17. cross-generation effects; subject mortality or multiple observations
18. cohort-sequential
19. cross-sectional; longitudinal

CHAPTER 10

USING SINGLE-SUBJECT DESIGNS

KEY QUESTIONS TO CONSIDER

- How were single-subject designs used in the early days of behavioral research?
- What are the major characteristics of the single-subject baseline design?
- What is a behavioral baseline and why is it important in a single-subject baseline design?
- What is a stability criterion, intrasubject replication, and intersubject replication?
- How does the baseline design differ from group-based designs?
- How does the baseline design handle random variability and error variance?
- How do you assess the reliability and the generality of findings from a single-subject baseline design?
- What strategies are used when implementing a baseline experiment?
- What are some of the problems faced when establishing baselines and how can these problems be handled?
- What are the characteristics of the single-factor baseline design?
- How do multifactor baseline designs work?
- What is a multiple baseline design and when would you use one?
- What does it mean to observe behavioral dynamics?
- What are the major characteristics of the discrete-trials design?
- How are inferential statistics used in single-subject designs?
- What are the advantages and disadvantages of the single-subject approach?

CHAPTER OUTLINE

A Little History
Baseline Versus Discrete Trials Designs
Baseline Designs
    Features of the Baseline Design
        The Behavioral Baseline

REVIEW AND STUDY QUESTIONS

Key Term Definition

Define each of the following terms.

Baseline design:

Baseline phase:

Intervention phase:

Behavioral baseline:

Stability criterion:

Intrasubject replication:

Intersubject replication:

Systematic variance:

Error variance:

Systematic replication:

Direct replication:

Reversal strategy:

ABA design:

ABAB design:

Multiple-baseline design:

Discrete trials design:

Multiple-Choice Questions

Circle the alternative that best completes the stem of each question.

1. The emphasis on developing laws of behavior that can be applied to individuals
   a. emerged only after sufficiently clear relationships had been identified via group experiments.
   b. has never been accepted within psychology.
   c. dates back to psychology's beginnings as an experimental discipline.
   d. has been discarded because of its impossibility.

2. Another name for the single-subject design is the
   a. small-*n* design.
   b. within-subjects design.
   c. repeated-measures design.
   d. between-subjects design.

3. When researchers refer to "single-subject designs," they usually mean
   a. within-subjects designs.
   b. between-subjects designs.
   c. baseline designs.
   d. discrete trials designs.

4. The essential feature of the baseline design is its use of
   a. a single subject.
   b. a behavioral baseline.
   c. inferential statistics.
   d. discrete trials.

5. The phase of a baseline experiment in which the treatment is introduced is the
   _____ phase.
   a. baseline
   b. intervention
   c. replication
   d. examination

6. The behavioral baseline serves to
   a. establish the level of the dependent variable under each phase of the experiment.
   b. assess the amount of uncontrolled variability present.
   c. provide the independent variable for the experiment.
   d. both a and b

7. The stability criterion is used in baseline designs to
   a. identify when the baseline no longer shows any systematic trends.
   b. determine when to move the subject to the next phase.
   c. determine when the value of the independent variable has become stable.
   d. both a and b

8. The only way to determine whether your stability criterion has been met is to
   a. conduct a statistical analysis on the baseline data.
   b. plot your data after each session and examine them.
   c. consult an astrologer.
   d. compute the standard error for the baseline data.

9. A successful intrasubject replication in a baseline experiment indicates that
   a. the results are probably reliable.
   b. the results will generalize to other subjects.
   c. the results will generalize to other species.
   d. all the above are true.

10. Single-subject baseline designs use _____ to establish the generality of findings across subjects.
    a. intersubject replication
    b. intrasubject replication
    c. random sampling
    d. extrasubject replication

11. A baseline design that involves establishing a baseline, then introducing a treatment, then reestablishing the baseline, and finally reintroducing the treatment
    a. would be termed an ABAB design.
    b. provides a built-in intrasubject replication for both the baseline and treatment conditions.
    c. in clinical treatment has the desirable property of ending with the treatment phase in effect.
    d. all of the above

12. If the baseline shows unacceptably high fluctuations over time within a condition, you should
    a. increase the number of subjects in the experiment.
    b. reduce the stability criterion.
    c. take steps to identify the factors responsible and control them.
    d. abandon the experiment.

13. Drifting baselines
    a. render a baseline experiment totally confounded.
    b. are desirable in baseline experiments.
    c. make a statistical analysis of the data mandatory.
    d. can be dealt with if the drift is relatively uniform over time.

14. When using multiple levels of the independent variable in a single-subject design,
    a. carryover effects are never a problem.
    b. you include enough subjects to completely counterbalance treatment order across subjects.
    c. you administer the various levels of the independent variable repeatedly to each subject while varying the order of presentation.
    d. you cannot conduct such a design; instead, you must use a within-subjects design.

15. Single-subject baseline designs
    a. are limited to investigating a single factor at a time.
    b. can be used to evaluate the effects of two or more independent variables and their interactions.
    c. cannot be used to investigate multiple dependent variables within a single experiment.
    d. all of the above

16. If the baseline is irreversible,
    a. you cannot use a single-subject design.
    b. a multiple-baseline design may be used to establish the effectiveness of the independent variable.
    c. you should increase the number of subjects.
    d. you should take up another vocation.

17. Single-subject discrete trials designs
    a. expose each subject once to all the conditions of the experiment.
    b. average across subjects within each treatment.
    c. within each treatment, average across multiple exposures of the same subject.
    d. do not use averaging to gain stability in treatment means.

18. The analysis of data from discrete trials single-subject experiments is usually determined by
    a. whether the data meet the assumptions of a parametric statistical test.
    b. a theory or model of the behavior being examined.
    c. the type of baseline.
    d. the number of subjects tested.

19. Standard inferential statistics may give misleading results when applied to data from single-subject discrete trials experiments because
    a. serial dependency may exist across adjacent observations within a treatment.
    b. scores from different subjects may be correlated.
    c. subjects are not randomly assigned to treatments.
    d. of experimenter bias.

20. The main advantage of the single-subject approach is its
    a. emphasis on statistical hypothesis testing.
    b. brevity.
    c. focus on controlling error variance.
    d. ability to eliminate carryover.

21. Single-subject designs may not be the best approach when
    a. subject variables having a large effect on the dependent variable cannot be controlled.
    b. subjects are available only for a brief period of time.
    c. treatment conditions cause irreversible changes in responses to the levels of the independent variable.
    d. all of the above

22. In a multiple-baseline design, treatments are applied
    a. to all baseline behaviors simultaneously.
    b. to each baseline behavior in sequence.
    c. only to some participants.
    d. only to some baseline behaviors.

Fill-In Questions

Fill in the blanks with the word or phrase that best completes each sentence.

1. Single-subject baseline designs *usually* employ about _____ subjects.

2. In the single-subject design, reliability of effects is assessed by means of _____
    _____.

3. The application of statistical techniques to the study of individual differences was pioneered by
    _____.

4. In the single-subject design, extensive observations made across time in the same treatment
    condition provide a stable _____ against which to assess changes in
    behavior.

5. In the single-subject baseline design, subjects usually remain in a given treatment condition
    until a particular _____ is met.

6. In the baseline design, _____ replication shows whether the results
    obtained with one subject are similar or dissimilar to those obtained with the others.

7. Between-subjects and within-subjects designs use inferential statistics to establish reliability of
    effects, whereas single-subject designs use _____.

8. The single-subject approach works best when your degree of control over sources of error vari-
    ance is _____ and the effect of your independent variable is _____.

9. In the single-subject baseline design, subjects are usually returned to the baseline condition
    after receiving the treatment. When you do this, you are employing a _____
    strategy.

10. A baseline that fails to return to pretreatment levels because the treatment has permanently
    altered the subject's responses is said to be _____.

11. _____ baseline designs provide a solution to the problem of irreversible
    changes in baseline.

12. In discrete trials designs, behavior measured over a series of discrete trials is
    _____ to provide a relatively stable index of behavior within a treatment.

13. When scores from adjacent observations within a treatment are more similar to each other than
    scores from more widely separated observations, the scores are said to exhibit
    _____.

Essay Questions

1. Summarize the history of single-subject (or small-*n*) designs.

2. Describe the logic of the single-subject baseline design. How does this design assess reliability? How does it assess external validity?

3. Describe three problem baselines and what can be done to deal with each.

4. Describe the discrete trials single-subject design. How does it differ from the baseline design? How does it differ from the within-subjects design?

5. Why is serial dependency a problem for single-subject discrete trials designs?

EXERCISING YOUR KNOWLEDGE

Analyzing a Single-Subject Baseline Experiment

The following data were collected from three subjects in an ABAB single-subject baseline design. Each score represents the number of lever-press responses made by a rat during a single experimental session. During the baseline condition, responses had no effect. During the treatment condition, each response produced a stimulus whose reinforcing value was being assessed in the experiment.

Subject A:	Baseline:	11,09,04
	Treatment:	05,08,12,24,52,74,89,86,87
	Baseline:	65,43,21,26,15,09,05,07
	Treatment:	56,87,91,84,88
Subject B:	Baseline:	21,15,4,7,3
	Treatment:	4,3,15,24,29,54,64,75,74,85,81,80
	Baseline:	43,21,32,34,22,15,7,5
	Treatment:	24,56,65,87,70,85,83,89
Subject C:	Baseline:	12,14,10
	Treatment:	14,25,75,90,93,92
	Baseline:	14,9,15
	Treatment:	90,89,93

During the experiment, subjects remained in each condition until a stability criterion was met in which points from three successive sessions fell within a 10-response band ([greatest–least] <= 10 responses). The maximum number of responses possible was 100.

Plot the data separately for each rat, with sessions along the x-axis of the graph and responses along the y-axis. Connect all points within each phase (for example, all points from the first baseline phase). What similarities do you see in the data across replications of the same phase for a given rat? What differences? Across rats?

Now replot the data, using only the last three data points from each phase (those that met the stability criterion). Plot the data from all three rats on a single graph, using circles to represent the data from Rat A, squares for Rat B, and triangles for Rat C. Were the intrasubject replications for each subject successful? Were the intersubject replications successful? What can you conclude about the effect of the treatment? A reinforcer increases the strength of a response, as indicated by a higher rate of responding. Was the stimulus introduced in the treatment phase a reinforcer?

Analyzing a Single-Participant Discrete Trials Experiment

In a signal-detection experiment, a participant received 200 trials of exposure to four seconds of "white" noise (broad-spectrum hissing and rumbling). On a random half of the trials, a brief (1/8th second) 2000-Hz tone was presented. Immediately after each trial, the participant indicated whether she thought the tone had been presented by responding either "yes" or "no." She then rated her degree of confidence in this decision, with a "1" indicating a "weak hunch," a "2" indicating "some confidence," and a "3" indicating "absolutely sure."

After the experiment, the yes–no and confidence-rating scales were combined to produce a single scale ranging from 1 (yes—absolutely sure) to 6 (no—absolutely sure). The number of responses in each category for the signal and noise trials was as follows:

Response Category

	1	2	3	4	5	6	Total
Signal	54	11	10	1	13	11	100
Noise	11	9	8	5	13	54	100

In the following table, fill in the numbers from response category 1 above. Add to these numbers the responses from category 2 and place these "running totals" under category 2 below. Continue this process for the other response categories. (The running totals for category 6 should both equal 100.)

Response Category

	1	2	3	4	5	6
Signal						
Noise						

Now divide each of the above scores by the row total (100), and place the results in the table below.

Response Category

	1	2	3	4	5	6
p(YES/Signal)						
P(YES/Noise)						

116

The numbers in the table indicate the probability of saying yes given that the signal was present ("hits") and the probability of saying yes given that only noise was present ("false alarms"). The different response categories represent the participant's willingness to say yes. For example, category 1 represents the case where the participant was willing to say yes only when absolutely certain she heard the signal. Category 2 includes these cases plus the cases where the participant was not sure but had "some confidence" that the signal was presented. Thus, higher scale values indicate a greater willingness to say yes when uncertain.

Plot the pairs of scores for each response category on the graph that follows.

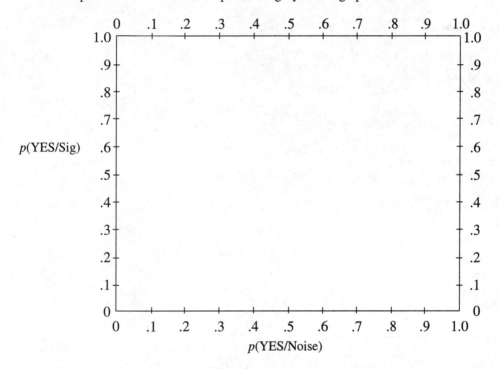

Draw a straight line connecting the lower left and upper right corners of the graph. This line (the "leading diagonal") indicates all points where the two probabilities are equal. Points falling along the leading diagonal indicate that the participant was unable to detect the signal. Now draw a smooth curve between the same two ends but running through the data points you plotted. The sensitivity of the participant to the signal is indicated by the degree to which the curve bows away from the leading diagonal. The position of each point along this curve indicates the participant's response bias, or willingness to say yes. Points near the origin (0, 0) indicate a conservative bias, whereas points near the upper right corner indicate a liberal bias. Was the participant sensitive to the stimulus?

ANSWERS TO QUESTIONS AND EXERCISES

Multiple-Choice Questions

1.	C	12.	C
2.	A	13.	D
3.	C	14.	C
4.	B	15.	B
5.	B	16.	B
6.	D	17.	C
7.	D	18.	B
8.	B	19.	A
9.	A	20.	C
10.	A	21.	D
11.	D	22.	B

Fill-In Questions

1. three to six
2. intrasubject replication
3. Francis Galton
4. baseline
5. stability criterion
6. intersubject
7. replication
8. high; large
9. reversal
10. irreversible
11. Multiple
12. averaged
13. serial dependency

CHAPTER 11

DESCRIBING DATA

KEY QUESTIONS TO CONSIDER

- Why is it important to scrutinize your data using exploratory data analysis (EDA)?
- How do you organize your data in preparation for data analysis?
- What are the advantages and disadvantages of analyzing grouped and individual data?
- How do various types of graphs differ and when should each be used?
- How do negatively accelerated, positively accelerated, and asymptotic functional relationships differ?
- Why is it important to graph your data?
- How do you graph a frequency distribution as a histogram? As a stemplot?
- What should you look for when examining the graph of a frequency distribution?
- How do the mode, median, and mean differ? Under what conditions would you use each?
- What measures of spread are available, and when would you use each?
- What is the five-number summary, and how can you represent it graphically?
- What do measures of association tell you?
- What factors affect the direction and magnitude of a correlation coefficient?
- What is linear regression, and how is it used to analyze data?
- How are the regression weights and standard error used to interpret the results from a multiple regression analysis?

CHAPTER OUTLINE

Descriptive Statistics and Exploratory Data Analysis
Organizing Your Data
    Organizing Your Data for Computer Entry
        Entering Your Data
    Grouped Versus Individual Data
        Grouped Data

Multivariate Correlational Techniques
Summary
Key Terms

REVIEW AND STUDY QUESTIONS

Key Term Definition

Define each of the following terms.

Exploratory data analysis (EDA):

Bar graph:

Line graph:

Scatterplot:

Pie chart:

Frequency distribution:

Histogram:

Stemplot:

Skewed distribution:

Normal distribution:

Outliers:

Resistant measures:

Mode:

Median:

Mean:

Range:

Interquartile range:

Variance:

Standard deviation:

Five-number summary:

Boxplot:

Pearson product–moment correlation coefficient, or Pearson *r:*

Point-biserial correlation:

Spearman rank order correlation (*rho*):

Linear regression:

Bivariate linear regression:

Least squares regression line:

Regression weight:

Standard error of estimate:

Multiple-Choice Questions

Circle the alternative that best completes the stem of each question.

1. Exploratory data analysis should be used to
   a. help you search for patterns in your data.
   b. spot serious defects in your data that may warrant taking corrective action.
   c. help determine whether assumptions of the inferential tests you intend to use may have been violated.
   d. all of the above

2. When data are copied to a computer coding sheet or into the computer data file, if the data are copied into the wrong column, this constitutes a(n) _____ error.
   a. transcription
   b. misplaced data
   c. dislocation
   d. alignment

3. A drawback to organizing data into groups is that
   a. the average performance of the group may not accurately represent the individual scores in the group.
   b. data organized in group form cannot be analyzed statistically.
   c. the average performance of the group usually overrepresents the individual scores in the group.
   d. both a and b

4. The horizontal axis of a graph is called the _____, whereas the vertical axis is called the
   _____.
   a. ordinate; abscissa
   b. y-axis; x-axis
   c. x-axis; y-axis
   d. linear; curvilinear

5. A bar graph is the best graph to use when
   a. your dependent variable was measured on at least a ratio scale.
   b. your independent variable is categorical.
   c. your independent and dependent variables are both continuous.
   d. you want to show ordered trends in your data.

6. To show a functional relationship between your independent and dependent variables, the graph of choice would be a
   a. line graph.
   b. histogram.
   c. pie chart.
   d. scatterplot.

7. A curve showing a functional relationship that starts off flat, becomes progressively steeper, and shows a single direction of change is
   a. negatively accelerated.
   b. monotonic.
   c. positively accelerated.
   d. both b and c

8. According to the text, graphing is important when
   a. deciding on an appropriate research strategy.
   b. your dependent variable was measured on at least a ratio scale.
   c. you cannot possibly describe your data in any other way.
   d. you are deciding on the appropriate descriptive statistic to apply to your data.

9. A _____ distribution has most scores collected about the center and is symmetrical about its midpoint.
   a. functional
   b. normal
   c. monotonic
   d. bimodal

10. A functional graph that shows a uniformly increasing or decreasing functional relationship is said to be
    a. monotonic.
    b. negatively skewed.
    c. normal.
    d. positively skewed.

11. An advantage of the stemplot for displaying a frequency distribution is that
    a. you can recover the actual score values from the plot.
    b. it automatically gives you the mean and standard deviation of the distribution.
    c. it allows you to use any class width you wish.
    d. all of the above

12. A _____ is used to provide a single score representing an entire distribution of scores.
    a. measure of correlation
    b. measure of center
    c. measure of spread
    d. summary statistic

13. The middle score in an ordered distribution is the
    a. mode.
    b. mean.
    c. median.
    d. interquartile mean.

14. While the range is the _____ measure of spread, it is also _____.
    a. most difficult to compute; the most informative
    b. easiest to compute; the least informative
    c. most preferred; the most difficult to compute
    d. none of the above

15. Dr. Jones measures how responsive a mother is to her infant by rating her behavior on a 10-point scale. He also obtains a measure of the strength of the infant's attachment to the mother. He finds that as maternal responsiveness increases so does the strength of the attachment. This is an example of a(n)
    a. negative correlation.
    b. inverse relationship.
    c. functional relationship.
    d. positive correlation.

16. In which of the following situations would you *not* want to use a Pearson correlation coefficient?
    a. When the relationship between variables is nonlinear
    b. When both of your variables are measured on at least an interval scale
    c. When the variances of your distributions are very similar
    d. You would not use the Pearson correlation in any of the above situations.

Fill-In Questions

Fill in the blanks with the word or phrase that best completes each sentence.

1. A curve that reaches a certain point and then levels off is said to be _____.

2. A curve that changes direction only once is _____.

3. The most frequent score in a distribution is the _____.

4. If your data were normally distributed and measured on at least an interval scale, the measure of center of choice is the _____.

5. The most popular measure of spread is the _____.

6. A correlation coefficient especially designed for use when one of your variables is dichotomous and the other continuous is the _____.

7. The sign of a correlation coefficient tells you something about the _____ _____ of the relationship between variables, whereas its magnitude tells you about the _____ of the relationship.

8. An outlying score can affect the magnitude of a correlation coefficient most severely when the correlation is based on _____.

9. The point-biserial correlation tends to underestimate the degree of relationship between variables because _____.

10. The formula for the least squares regression line is _____.

11. The amount of error in prediction in a linear regression analysis is given by the
_____.

12. $1 - r^2$ is the formula for the _____.

13. A table that shows the intercorrelations among a set of variables is a(n) _____
_____.

14. _____ is used when you want to look at the relationships among three or more variables simultaneously.

Essay Questions

1. Explain why it is a good idea, where possible, to evaluate individual as well as grouped data.

2. List and discuss the four major measures of center. How is each computed? Order them in terms of how much information is provided and indicate when you might want to use each.

3. Do the same for the measures of spread as you did for the measures of center in question 2.

4. Discuss each of the factors cited in the text that affect the magnitude and/or direction of the Pearson correlation coefficient.

EXERCISING YOUR KNOWLEDGE

Measures of Center

Here are two distributions of scores. For each, do the following:
1. Plot a frequency distribution, and identify it as either normal or skewed (you can do this visually).
2. Calculate the mode, median, and mean. Indicate on the appropriate frequency distribution where each falls.
3. Determine which measure of center is appropriate for each distribution and why.
   Distribution 1:   1, 3, 2, 5, 3, 3, 4, 1, 4, 3, 3, 2, 5, 3, 2, 4, 3, 3, 2, 2
   Distribution 2:   5, 5, 4, 4, 4, 3, 2, 2, 1, 3, 4, 5, 4, 5, 5, 5, 4, 3, 5, 5

Using the Pearson Correlation Coefficient

The text discusses the Pearson correlation coefficient extensively. This exercise will help you understand more about the correct application of this common statistic. Following are two sets of scores. For each do the following:

1. Compute a Pearson correlation coefficient for each set of scores. (You can use the Statistical Analysis Package that your instructor has. Ask him or her for a copy.) Obtain the Pearson r, and relevant means and standard deviations.

2. Plot the scores from each set on a separate scatterplot. Inspect the scatterplot to see if the data met the assumptions of the Pearson correlation coefficient analysis.

3. Compare the correlation coefficients that you obtained, and inspect your scatterplots. Can you think of any reasons why the correlation coefficients differed the way they did? Is the Pearson correlation coefficient appropriate for both sets of scores? Why or why not?

Set 1		Set 2	
X	Y	X	Y
1	1	1	2
1	2	2	3
2	1	3	5
2	2	2	1
2	4	3	4
3	4	4	5
3	5	6	7
4	7	6	6
5	7	3	2
5	4	7	5
5	5	4	3
6	4	7	7
6	2	5	5
6	1	3	1
7	1	5	6

ANSWERS TO QUESTIONS AND EXERCISES

Multiple-Choice Questions

1.	D	9.	B
2.	B	10.	A
3.	A	11.	A
4.	C	12.	D
5.	B	13.	C
6.	A	14.	B
7.	D	15.	D
8.	D	16.	A

Fill-In Questions

1. asymptotic
2. monotonic
3. mode
4. mean
5. standard deviation
6. point-biserial correlation
7. direction; strength
8. a small number of pairs of scores
9. the range of the dichotomous variable is restricted
10. $Y' = BX + $ constant
11. standard error of estimate
12. coefficient of nondetermination
13. correlation matrix
14. Multivariate analysis

Exercising Your Knowledge

Measures of Center

Distribution 1:

1. This distribution approximates a normal distribution.
2. $\overline{X} = 2.9$
   Median = 3
   Mode = 3
3. The mean is most appropriate.

Distribution 2:

1. This distribution is negatively skewed.
2. $\overline{X} = 3.90$
   Median = 4
   Mode = 5
3. The mean does not provide an accurate representation of the scores. Therefore the mode or median should be used.

Using the Pearson Correlation Coefficient

Set 1:

1. $r = .13, \overline{X} = 3.87, \overline{Y} = 3.33, S_x = 1.99, S_y = 2.09$

2. The scatterplot of these data shows a curvilinear relationship between X and Y.

Set 2:

1. $r = .81$, $\overline{X} = 4.07$, $\overline{Y} = 4.13$, $S_x = 1.87$, $S_y = 2.03$

2. The scatterplot of these data shows a linear relationship between X and Y.

3. Comparing the two coefficients, it is evident that the correlation for set 1 is much lower than the one for set 2. An inspection of the scatterplots, however, shows that the relationship between X and Y for set 1 is nonlinear. Obviously, there is a relationship between X and Y for set 1. The Pearson correlation coefficient underestimates the degree of relationship between the scores in sets 1 and 2.

CHAPTER 12

USING INFERENTIAL STATISTICS

KEY QUESTIONS TO CONSIDER

- Why are sampling distributions important in inferential statistics?
- What is sampling error and why is it important to know about?
- What are degrees of freedom and how do they relate to inferential statistics?
- How do parametric and nonparametric statistics differ?
- What is the general logic behind inferential statistics?
- How are Type I and Type II errors related?
- What is the meaning of "statistical significance"?
- When should you use a two-tailed test?
- What are the assumptions underlying parametric statistics?
- Which parametric statistics would you use to analyze data from an experiment with two groups? Identify which test would be used for a particular type of design or data.
- Which parametric statistic is most appropriate for designs with more than one level of a single independent variable?
- When would you do a "planned" comparison versus an "unplanned" comparison, and why?
- What is the difference between a weighted and unweighted means analysis? When would you use either?
- What is a "main effect" and an "interaction" and how are they analyzed?
- Under what conditions would you use a nonparametric statistic?
- What is meant by the "power" of a statistical test and what factors can affect it?
- Does a statistically significant finding always have practical significance?
- When are data transformations used?
- What are the alternatives to inferential statistics for evaluating the reliability of data?

CHAPTER OUTLINE

Inferential Statistics: Basic Concepts
    Sampling Distribution
    Sampling Error
    Degrees of Freedom
    Parametric Versus Nonparametric Statistics
The Logic Behind Inferential Statistics
    Statistical Errors
    Statistical Significance
    One-Tailed Versus Two-Tailed Tests
Parametric Statistics
    Assumptions Underlying a Parametric Statistic
    Inferential Statistics With Two Samples
    The t Test
        The t Test for Independent Samples
        The t Test for Correlated Samples
        Contrasting Two Groups: An Example From the Literature
        The z Test for the Difference Between Two Proportions
    Beyond Two Groups: Analysis of Variance (ANOVA)
        Partitioning Variation
        The F Ratio
    The One-Factor Between-Subjects ANOVA
        Interpreting Your F Ratio
        Planned Comparisons
        Unplanned Comparisons
        Sample Size
        Unweighted Means Analysis
        Weighted Means Analysis
    The One-Factor Within-Subjects ANOVA
        The Latin Square ANOVA
        Interpreting Your F Ratio
    The Two-Factor Between-Subjects ANOVA
        Main Effects and Interactions
        Sample Size
        ANOVA for a Two-Factor Between-Subjects Design: An Example
        Interpreting the Results
    The Two-Factor Within-Subjects ANOVA
    Mixed Designs
    Higher Order and Special Case ANOVAs
Nonparametric Statistics
    Chi-Square

REVIEW AND STUDY QUESTIONS

Key Term Definition

Define each of the following terms.

Inferential statistics:

Standard error of the mean:

Degrees of freedom:

Type I error:

Type II error:

Alpha level:

Critical region:

t test for independent samples:

t test for correlated samples:

132

z test for the difference between two proportions:

Analysis of variance (ANOVA):

F ratio:

p value:

Planned comparison:

Unplanned comparison:

Per-comparison error:

Familywise error:

Chi-square:

Mann–Whitney U test:

Power:

Effect size:

Data transformation:

Multiple-Choice Questions

Circle the alternative that best completes the stem of each question.

1. If you drew every possible sample of a given size from a population and calculated a mean for each sample, the distribution of those means is the
   a. sampling distribution of the mean.
   b. standard error of the mean.
   c. degrees of freedom of the mean.
   d. central tendency of the mean.

2. An assumption underlying parametric statistics is that
    a. sampling was done from a normally distributed population.
    b. your data were measured on an interval or ratio scale.
    c. your data need not meet any strict requirements.
    d. both a and b

3. If your independent variable has no effect on the dependent variable, the distributions representing the different groups in your experiment
    a. represent two distinct populations.
    b. are independent samples drawn from the same population.
    c. are probably positively skewed.
    d. are probably negatively skewed.

4. The hypothesis that says that your sample means were drawn from the same population is the
    a. alternative hypothesis.
    b. central limit hypothesis.
    c. null hypothesis.
    d. post hoc hypothesis.

5. If the probability that the difference between sample means could have resulted by sampling the same population is sufficiently small, then we say that the difference between means is
    a. not statistically significant.
    b. statistically significant.
    c. valid.
    d. none of the above

6. Although inferential statistics are designed to help you minimize decision-making errors, errors are still possible. If you decided to reject the null hypothesis when in fact it was true, you are making a
    a. Type II error.
    b. Type I error.
    c. Type III error.
    d. per-comparison error.

7. If you take steps to minimize a Type I error, then the probability of making a Type II error is
    a. increased.
    b. also decreased.
    c. unaffected.
    d. cut in half.

8. By convention, alpha has been set at no larger than $p <$
    a. .10.
    b. .05.
    c. .025.
    d. .01.

9. According to the text, one-tailed tests should be used
   a. whenever you are unsure what kind of test to use.
   b. in any situation where you cannot predict the direction of an effect.
   c. only if there is some compelling a priori reason not to use a two-tailed test.
   d. when nonparametric statistics are used.

10. The most appropriate statistical test for an experiment with two groups and the dependent variable measured on an interval scale is
    a. the chi-square.
    b. the t test for independent samples.
    c. the one-sample z test.
    d. a two-factor ANOVA.

11. For an experimental design that goes beyond two groups and a dependent variable measured on an interval scale, the best statistic is the
    a. ANOVA.
    b. t test for correlated samples.
    c. Mann–Whitney U test.
    d. chi-square test.

12. If you are contemplating doing many post hoc, unplanned comparisons, you must be concerned with
    a. per-comparison error.
    b. beta errors.
    c. familywise error.
    d. probability funneling.

13. If you have unequal sample sizes, you would use an unweighted means analysis if
    a. your experimental procedure caused the unequal sample sizes.
    b. your experimental procedure did not cause the unequal sample sizes.
    c. the size of the sample in one group did not exceed any of the others by more than three participants.
    d. both a and b

14. Nonparametric tests
    a. are used only when your data do not meet the assumptions of parametric statistics.
    b. are used if your data do not meet the assumptions of a parametric test, even if your data were scaled on an interval or ratio scale.
    c. are used when your data are scaled on less than an interval scale.
    d. both b and c

15. The power of a statistical test refers to its
    a. ability to eliminate statistical errors.
    b. ability to analyze data that violate the assumptions of the test.
    c. ability to detect differences between means.
    d. all of the above

Fill-In Questions

Fill in the blanks with the word or phrase that best completes each sentence.

1. According to the _____, a distribution of sample means will approximate a normal distribution even if the distribution of scores from the population is skewed.

2. The number of scores that are free to vary in a sample of a given size with a known mean is known as the _____.

3. _____ statistics assume that data are normally distributed and scaled on at least an interval scale.

4. If you decided not to reject the null hypothesis and it was, in fact, false, you have committed a _____ error.

5. The _____ that you adopt is really the probability that the observed difference between your sample means could have occurred purely through sampling error.

6. List two of the three assumptions underlying parametric statistics:

    1. _____

    2. _____

7. In the analysis of variance, the total variance is partitioned into _____ and _____.

8. If you have specific, preexperimental hypotheses about which of your multiple groups differ, you can forgo an overall ANOVA in favor of _____.

9. _____ is the error rate that takes into account the probability of making at least one Type I error as the number of comparisons increases.

10. A(n) _____ is said to exist if the impact of one independent variable differs over levels of a second.

11. According to the text, two drawbacks to using nonparametric statistics are _____ _____ and _____ .

12. Reducing alpha (for example, from .05 to .01) leads to a(n) _____ _____ in power.

13. _____ tells you the probability of your findings if chance alone is operating, whereas _____ refers to how "important" your findings are.

14. A(n) _____ changes the magnitude of the numbers in a distribution but not the scale of measurement.

15. Some researchers advocate the use of _____ as a reason- able substitute for inferential statistics for testing the reliability of data.

Essay Questions

1. Discuss the "logic behind inferential statistics." Specifically, how does an inferential statistic allow you to make inferences about the population or populations from which your samples are drawn?

2. Discuss the role of statistical errors in decision making. Define the two types of errors and how each might be controlled.

3. Compare and contrast one-tailed and two-tailed statistics. What factors affect your decision to use one over the other? How does your decision influence the probability of obtaining a "sta- tistically significant" effect?

4. What is power, why is it important, and what affects it?

5. What does a large effect size indicate? A small one?

6. Compare and contrast practical and statistical significance.

7. What are data transformations, and when would you use them?

EXERCISING YOUR KNOWLEDGE

Which Statistic Applies?

Here are descriptions of three published research studies. For each, identify the appropriate statistical test to apply. In all cases assume that the data meet the assumptions underlying parametric statistics.

1. To see if there is an age-related change in altruism in children, Grunberg, Maycock, and Anthony (1985) measured the number of pennies children donated to UNICEF when left alone. Participants were classified into six age groups (3–4, 5–6, 7–8, 9–10, 11–12, 13–16) and given an opportunity to donate any or all of 10 pennies given to them by the experimenter.

2. Thompson (1982) wanted to know if keeping a diary was a behavior that is more typical of females than males. He administered a questionnaire to 148 students in an introductory psychology class. The number of men and women keeping and not keeping a diary was recorded and analyzed.

3. Hall (1982) investigated the effects of list organization and distraction on memory. The independent variables were list type (organized or unorganized) and the type of distractor (similar to the original words or unrelated to the original words) included during the recognition test. Each of eighty participants was randomly assigned to one of the four experimental conditions. The number of words from the original list that were recognized was the dependent variable.

Sources

Grunberg, N. E., Maycock, V. A., & Anthony, B. J. (1985). Material altruism in children. *Basic and Applied Social Psychology, 6,* 1–12.

Hall, J. F. (1982). List organization and recognition memory. *Bulletin of the Psychonomic Society, 20,* 35–36.

Thompson, C. P. (1982). Diary-keeping as a sex-role behavior. *Bulletin of the Psychonomic Society, 20,* 11–13.

Calculating an ANOVA

The analysis of variance is the most widely used statistic for factorial designs employing a dependent variable scaled on at least an interval scale. This exercise will give you practice calculating and interpreting an ANOVA.

Here are some data to analyze. Assume that the design was a completely between-participants factorial. Conduct an ANOVA (using LabStat or another statistical analysis package). Answer the following questions:

1. Which effects were statistically significant and at what p value?

2. Would you interpret the main effects in the light of the way the interaction turned out? Why or why not?

IV1: Level 1		IV1: Level 2	
IV2: Level 1	IV2: Level 2	IV2: Level 1	IV2: Level 2
3	3	3	1
5	3	6	1
2	4	4	2
1	2	2	1
3	3	3	0

Multiple-Choice Questions

1.	A	9.	C
2.	D	10.	B
3.	B	11.	A
4.	C	12.	C
5.	B	13.	B
6.	B	14.	D
7.	A	15.	C
8.	B		

Fill-In Questions

1. central limit theorem
2. degrees of freedom
3. Parametric
4. beta or Type II
5. alpha level
6. sampling was done from a normally distributed population; within-group variances are homogeneous; sampling was random
7. between-groups variance; within-groups variance
8. planned comparisons
9. Familywise error
10. interaction
11. less sensitivity than parametric statistics; difficulty analyzing complex designs
12. reduction
13. Statistical significance; practical significance
14. linear transformation
15. replication

Exercising Your Knowledge

Which Statistic Applies?

1. The dependent variable in this study was the number of pennies donated and was scaled on a ratio scale. The "independent" variable was age category. The most appropriate statistic is a one-factor, between-subjects analysis of variance.

2. In this study the researchers counted the number of males and females falling into each category (diary versus no diary). The most appropriate statistic for this study is chi-square.

3. There were two independent variables (list type and distractor type) and a continuously measured dependent variable (number of words correctly recognized). Because participants received only one of the four treatments, the design of this study is a 2×2 between-subjects factorial. Consequently, the appropriate statistic is a two-factor, between-subjects analysis of variance.

Cell, Row, and Column Means

IV1

		Level 1	Level 2	
IV2	Level 1	2.8	3.6	3.2
	Level 2	3.0	1.0	2.0
		2.9	2.3	

ANOVA Table

Source of Variance	Sum of Squares	Degrees of Freedom	Mean Square	F	p
IV1	1.80	1	1.80	1.31	N.S.
IV2	7.20	1	7.20	5.24	$< .05$
IV1 $\times$ IV2	9.80	1	9.80	7.13	$< .025$
Error	22.00	16	1.38		

1. The main effect of IV2 was statistically significant at $p < .05$, and the interaction of IV1 and IV2 was statistically significant at $p < .025$.

2. Interpreting the main effect of IV1 would be misleading because of the presence of the interaction. There is no simple effect of IV1. Instead, the impact of IV1 on the dependent variable depends on the level of IV2.

CHAPTER 13

REPORTING YOUR RESEARCH RESULTS

KEY QUESTIONS TO CONSIDER

- How do you set up a paper using APA writing style?
- What is the heading style used in an APA-style manuscript?
- What information is included on the title page, and in what order would you find that information (from the top to the bottom of the page)?
- What are the differences between a running head and a manuscript page header?
- What is an abstract and why is it so important?
- What information goes into an abstract and how long should an abstract be?
- What information is included in the introduction to an APA-style paper? How is the introduction organized?
- What information would you expect to find in the method section? Describe the various subsections of the method section.
- What would you expect to find in the results section of a manuscript?
- How is the results section formatted and how are statistics reported?
- How is the discussion section of a manuscript organized, and what would you expect to find in the discussion section?
- When do you include author notes and footnotes in an APA-style manuscript? Where should they be placed?
- How are the tables used in an APA-style manuscript formatted? When are tables used?
- How is a page containing a figure set up? When are figures used?
- What is included in the reference list of an APA-style manuscript? Describe how a typical journal reference is formatted.
- What are the general rules for using numbers in the text of a manuscript?
- What is biased language and how can you avoid using it?
- Why are clarity of expression, organization, and style so important to consider when preparing a manuscript? What comprises each?
- What are plagiarism and lazy writing and how can you avoid them?

- What is typically the sequence of events involved in submitting a paper for publication?
- What is the difference between an oral presentation and a poster session?

CHAPTER OUTLINE

APA Writing Style
Writing an APA-Style Paper
    Getting Ready to Type
        Formatting a Page
        Heading Structure
    The Title Page
        Title
        Author Name(s) and Affiliation(s)
        Running Head
    The Abstract
        Formatting the Abstract
    The Introduction
        Formatting the Introduction
    The Method Section
        Subjects or Participants
        Apparatus or Materials
        Procedure
        Combining Sections
        Formatting the Method Section
    The Results Section
        Formatting the Results Section
    The Discussion Section
    The Reference Section
    Other Optional Information
        Author Notes
        Footnotes
        Tables
        Figure Captions
        Figures
    Citing References in Your Report
    Using Numbers in the Text
    Avoiding Biased Language
Expression, Organization, and Style
    Expressing Your Ideas Clearly
        Grammatical Correctness
        Proper Word Choice
        Economy of Expression

REVIEW AND STUDY QUESTIONS

Key Term Definition

Define each of the following terms.

Manuscript page header:

Running head:

Abstract:

Introduction:

Method section:

Subjects subsection:

Participants subsection:

Apparatus subsection:

Materials subsection:

Procedure subsection:

Results section:

Discussion section:

Reference section:

Plagiarism:

Lazy writing:

Paper presentation:

Multiple-Choice Questions

Circle the alternative that best completes the stem of each question.

1. The final step in the research process is to
   a. conduct a statistical analysis of the data.
   b. report the research results.
   c. dismantle the apparatus.
   d. clean the laboratory.

2. Learning how to write a research report is valuable
   a. only if you are going to become a scientist.
   b. only if you are going to become an experimental psychologist.
   c. only if you are planning to become a writer.
   d. for any occupation where you will have to organize facts, draw logical conclusions, and present those facts and conclusions to others.

3. When you write a research report for submission to an APA journal, the report must conform to
   a. APA writing style.
   b. the style of the American Physical Society.
   c. the factual and ethical standards of the *National Enquirer.*
   d. all of the above

4. Which of the following is true?
   a. All psychology journals require strict adherence to APA writing style.
   b. Only APA journals follow APA writing style.
   c. Non-APA journals usually follow APA writing style with minor changes.
   d. Non-APA journals usually follow a style very different from APA writing style.

5. Manuscripts that follow APA style must be
   a. single-spaced.
   b. double-spaced.
   c. triple-spaced.
   d. trimmed in gold leaf.

6. To be effective, the title of your article should be
    a. long so that all important details of the study can be indicated.
    b. short and cute.
    c. concise, yet informative.
    d. peppered with long words.

7. A shortened title that will appear at the top of each page in the published article is the
    a. article title.
    b. running head.
    c. by-line.
    d. abstract.

8. An abstract for a research report should not exceed
    a. 50 words.
    b. 120 words.
    c. 150 words.
    d. 25 lines.

9. The primary function of the introduction is to
    a. provide an exhaustive review of the literature on the topic covered by the research.
    b. entertain the reader.
    c. justify the study described in the report.
    d. describe the conclusions drawn from the results of the research.

10. The structure of the introduction proceeds
    a. from the general to the specific.
    b. from the specific to the general.
    c. from general to specific and back to general again.
    d. from general question to the results of the research.

11. When writing the introduction, you should assume that
    a. the reader knows nothing about the topic.
    b. the reader knows everything about the topic.
    c. the reader has some knowledge of the basic psychological concepts that underlie your study.
    d. the editors of the journal will fill in any missing details for you.

12. The proper place to describe how your questionnaire was organized would be in the
    a. introduction.
    b. procedure section.
    c. materials section.
    d. discussion section.

13. The method section of your research report should
    a. describe everything concerning your participants, apparatus, and procedure that you can think of.
    b. provide enough information about your study that the reader could duplicate it in all its essential details.
    c. tell what mistakes you made in your pilot study that you eliminated in the actual study.
    d. discuss the results of your study.

14. When presenting the results of a statistical analysis of your data, you should usually
    a. put them in a table showing the sources of variance, sums of squares, mean squares, F ratios, and probability values.
    b. indicate which differences in treatment means were statistically significant but not describe what the means actually were.
    c. state in sentence form what comparison is being evaluated, whether or not the difference was statistically significant, the critical statistic and its degrees of freedom, the value obtained for the statistic, and the level of significance achieved.
    d. all of the above

15. The correct citation format for reporting the results from an analysis of variance is
    a. $F(85) = 7.98, p < .05$
    b. $F(1, 85) = 7.98, p > .95$
    c. $F(1, 85) = 7.98, p < .05$
    d. $F = 7.98, p < .05$

16. Interpretation of your results belongs in the
    a. introduction.
    b. method section.
    c. results section.
    d. discussion section.

17. The reference section of your research report should contain a listing of all the references that
    a. were cited in the report.
    b. you read when preparing to write the report.
    c. you believe the readers of your report would find useful.
    d. have anything at all to do with the topic of your report.

18. The purpose of the discussion section is to
    a. explain why the results of your study don't really mean anything.
    b. interpret the results and indicate how they fit with previous research and theory.
    c. justify the study.
    d. list all the things that went wrong as you attempted to carry out the study.

19. On a graph, the levels of the independent variable are usually represented on the
    a. x-axis.
    b. y-axis.
    c. ordinate.
    d. figure caption.

20. Which of the following sentences is grammatically incorrect?
    a. The independent variable was found to effect the dependent variable.
    b. The data from the experiment is presented in Figure 1.
    c. The affect of the independent variable was minimal.
    d. all of the above

21. After you submit your paper to a journal for review, you may have to wait _____
    before you receive your first feedback.
    a. as much as two weeks
    b. a month
    c. two months or more
    d. several years

22. When giving an oral presentation of your research results, you should
    a. provide an informal description, organized "on the spot."
    b. read your paper from typed notes.
    c. develop an outline of your talk and stick to it.
    d. give all the details of your methodology.

23. The main advantage of the poster session over an oral presentation is that
    a. you can engage in meaningful conversations with other people who are doing research in your area.
    b. you can communicate to a larger number of people in a short time.
    c. you do not have to spend as much time preparing.
    d. you are limited to less than 15 minutes.

24. The _____ sentence (usually the first in a paragraph) conveys the topic of the paragraph to your reader.
    a. theme
    b. support
    c. limiting
    d. transitional

25. A number in a sentence should be spelled out when it
    a. begins the sentence.
    b. is 10 or under.
    c. appears in a hyphenated expression.
    d. all of the above

Fill-In Questions

Fill in the blanks with the word or phrase that best completes each sentence.

1. Scientific journals specify the format, or _____, that submitted articles are to follow.

2. The author name(s) and affiliation(s) appear on the _____ of the research manuscript.

3. The first two or three words of your title are used for the _____.

4. The _____ is a concise summary of your paper.

5. In the _____ of your research paper, you provide a brief review of the relevant literature on the topic.

6. The only section of your paper that does not include a heading indicating the name of the section is the _____.

7. If your study uses an unconventional or complex design, you may include a separate _____ subsection in the method section to describe it.

8. If your study made use of questionnaires rather than laboratory equipment, you would include a _____ subsection instead of an apparatus subsection.

9. Demographic information about your participants would usually be presented in the _____ subsection.

10. The _____ subsection describes precisely what procedure was followed throughout the course of your study.

11. The purpose of your _____ section is to report what you found.

12. In the discussion section you _____ your results and _____ _____.

13. Any articles or books you cited in the body of your paper *must* be listed in the _____ section.

14. _____ can be used to illustrate the design and materials of your study and to present data.

15. Graphs, drawings, and photographs are three commonly used types of _____
    _____.

16. The _____ of a graph tells your reader what each of the points and lines on the graph means.

17. When there are three or more authors of a paper, you can save effort in writing the names by using the _____ convention for the second and subsequent citations of the article.

18. _____ sentences follow the theme sentence and support and elaborate the theme.

19. If you use someone else's words or ideas without proper citation, you are guilty of _____.

20. The two types of paper presentations are _____ presentations and _____.

Essay Questions

1. Describe what information should be included in the abstract of a research report. What should be excluded?

2. List the parts usually contained in the introduction to a research report.

3. What information goes in the results section, and what goes in the discussion section? Under what conditions might it be a good idea to combine these sections?

4. Describe the elements of clarity of expression, organization, and style. Why is it important to pay attention to these factors?

5. What is biased language in writing, and how can you avoid using the problem?

6. What are the four general rules suggested by Crews (1980) to help you achieve unity within paragraphs?

7. Describe what sequence of events takes place when you submit your research paper to a journal for publication.

EXERCISING YOUR KNOWLEDGE

Analyzing a Manuscript

The following "manuscript" badly needs revision to correct various errors of organization, style, and format. Make the necessary changes by marking them on the manuscript.

The Affect of Retention Interval on

Short-term Memory

by

Ebbinghaus Jones, State University

RUNNING HEAD: Affect

Abstract

Memory for dental appointments was assessed at retention intervals of 3, 6, 12, 15, and 18 seconds. Ten subjects were tested individually in a small cubicle with the door closed. The intervals used ranged from 3 to 18 seconds and memory was assessed at each interval using a stopwatch that had an accuracy of 1/100th second. Subjects were required to perform mental arithmetic during the retention interval to prevent them from rehearsing the appointments. The results were very significant and could provide the basis for further research. An additional experiment showed that dental appointments were forgotten more rapidly than nonsense syllables, suggesting that subjects had repressed the dental appointments.

Introduction

Research indicates that recall of consonant trigrams (e.g., KJG) declines sharply as a function of retention interval if rehearsal is prevented, Peterson and Peterson, 1959. Most people have trouble remembering appointments, especially dental appointments. An important question is whether memory for dental appointments declines over time at the same rate as memory for consonant trigrams. The present study did this.

Method

Subjects

10 volunteers from an introductory psychology class participated. For course credit. Their names were Sue, Fred, John, Bill, Alice, Janet, Stephanie, George, Jim, and Kelly. Two of the subjects were blonds, the rest had brown hair.

Apparatus

A stopwatch. It was used to time the retention intervals. Testing took place in a small cubicle normally used by students for studying. The door on the cubicle had a Yale lock, and the floor was tiled.

Subjects were tested individually in the cubicle. The experimenter told each subject that he or she would be given a dental appointment, followed immediately by a three-digit number. The subject was instructed to mentally subtract three from the number, then subtract three from the result, and continue in this fashion until the buzzer sounded. At the sound of the buzzer the subject was instructed to repeat the dental appointment that had been given at the beginning.

Procedure

Each subject was tested once at each of six retention intervals, ranging from 3 to 18 seconds in 3-second increments. I think it was a within-subjects design. The order of treatments was counterbalanced across subjects. All the subjects were very enthusiastic. When the subject was over, he or she was thanked for participating. The experimenter recorded the number of dental appointments correctly recalled after each trial.

Results

The results were very interesting. Table 1 shows them.

Insert Figure 1 about here

As you can see in the aforementioned Table 1 (see above), subjects' recall of the dental appointments worsened as the retention interval was lengthened. A one-way analysis of variance for trend showed some significance. The Mean Square was 443.23, F was 8.345 and this was for 1 degree of freedom in the numerator and 8 in the denominator, giving a p less than 0.05.

This means that there definitely was an effect of retention interval and not just the null hypothesis. Future experiments could test whether other appointments (e.g., doctor, haircut) produce similar results.

Identifying Biased Language

Go to the library and look up two or three articles from the past four decades (1950s to date), and analyze them for instances of biased language. Do you see any changes in the language used by authors of the articles? What have authors done to reduce biased language?

ANSWERS TO QUESTIONS AND EXERCISES

Multiple-Choice Questions

1.	B	6.	C	11.	C	16.	D	21.	C
2.	D	7.	B	12.	C	17.	A	22.	C
3.	A	8.	B	13.	B	18.	B	23.	A
4.	C	9.	C	14.	C	19.	A	24.	A
5.	B	10.	A	15.	C	20.	D	25.	D

Fill-In Questions

1. writing style
2. title page
3. manuscript page header
4. abstract
5. introduction
6. introduction
7. design
8. materials
9. participants
10. procedure
11. results
12. interpret; draw conclusions
13. reference
14. Tables
15. figures
16. legend
17. et al.
18. Support
19. plagiarism
20. oral; poster sessions

Exercising Your Knowledge

There were of course a few things wrong with the example research "paper." Here is a list of the ones we found, organized according to section:

Title page

The word "affect" is wrong and should be changed to "effect" in both the title and running head. The title itself is vague (short-term memory for what?). The university affiliation should appear beneath the author's name, and the word "by" should be omitted. The running head is too short to be descriptive. The manuscript page header and page number are missing.

Abstract

The procedure is described in too much detail, and some information is repeated. The intervals used could be summarized as "ranging from 3 to 18 seconds" in the first sentence. The second and third sentences should be eliminated to avoid repetition of the intervals used and to delete the information about where testing took place, how the intervals were timed, and the accuracy of the stopwatch. "Subjects" should be referred to as "participants."

Not enough information is given about the results (in fact, all you learn about them is that they were "very significant," which itself is poor usage; results are either significant or they are not). The abstract should summarize the important findings. The statement about the findings possibly providing the basis for further research is a generality that could apply to any study; it should be deleted. Finally, the abstract mentions an "additional experiment" that is not described anywhere else in the report. As a summary of the report's contents, the abstract should not introduce new material. The manuscript page header and page number are missing.

Introduction

The heading "Introduction" should not appear in the report. Replace it with the centered title of the paper. In the first sentence, the Peterson and Peterson (1959) study is cited improperly. Strike the comma after the word "prevented," and enclose the citation (including date) in parentheses. The assertion about most people having "trouble remembering dental appointments" should be supported by reference to an appropriate citation or to common experience. The "important question" mentioned was not the one tested by the reported experiment, because only dental appointments were used. The statement that the "present study did this" is not only false, it is vague and has no referent (did what?). This sentence should indicate what was tested, including mention of both the independent and dependent variables. The manuscript page header and page number are missing.

Method

The *Subjects* subsection should be titled *Participants* because humans were employed in the study. Throughout the paper the term "participants" should replace "subjects." Also, the number 10 should be spelled out because it begins the sentence. The phrase "for course credit" is not a complete sentence and should be tacked on to the previous sentence. The names of the participants and the colors of their hair are irrelevant and should be omitted. The range of ages of the participants should be indicated and the mix of sexes.

In the *Apparatus* subsection, the period after the word "stopwatch" and the "It" from the next sentence should be removed in order to form a single, complete sentence. The information about the lock on the door and the floor covering is irrelevant detail and should be deleted. The entire last paragraph describes procedure and should be eliminated from the section. Finally, indirect reference is made to a buzzer. A sentence should state directly that a buzzer was used to signal the end of each retention interval.

In the *Procedure* section, a step-by-step description of the procedure should be given. Probably the best way to organize this one would be to present an overview (the participant was brought into the cubicle, was given instructions, received 80 trials of testing with order of trials counterbalanced across participants, was thanked for participating) followed by the details of presenting each trial (participants were given the trigram, then a number, were required to subtract aloud by threes from this number, and so on). In the section as currently written, the writer should be able to state that a within-subjects design was used, not guess about it. The fact that the participants were enthusiastic is not relevant to the procedure, and reference to it should be deleted. The sentence beginning "When the subject was over" has the wrong actor. It should state "When the *experiment* was over, the *participant* was thanked for participating." Finally, the last sentence refers to the wrong variable and is ambiguous concerning when the experimenter recorded the data. The experimenter recorded not the number of dental appointments, but whether the response was correct.

Results

The heading should be centered. Whether the results were interesting is a judgment better left to the reader. Reference to Table 1 should describe what the table shows ("Table 1 shows the percentage of dental appointments correctly recalled at each retention interval."). Repeating this reference to Table 1 ("aforementioned Table 1"; "see above") is unnecessary and distracting. The sentence should begin with the word "Participants."

The notation indicating where a figure or table should be placed is no longer used in the current APA writing style. Instead, the author should make specific references to any figures or tables. However, the author should not refer to the table as being "above" or "below." The manuscript page header and page number are missing.

A statistical test produces results that are either significant or not significant. The test does not "show significance," and there cannot be "some" of it. The information relating the numerical values associated with the test is presented in a nonstandard format and fails to indicate what differences were being tested for statistical significance. The following would be an acceptable improvement: "An analysis of variance for trend revealed a significant linear component, $F(1, 8) = 8.345$, $p < .05$."

The statement beginning "This means" is grammatically incorrect and should be restated to express the relationship found. It might read, "Memory for dental appointments thus showed a reliable linear decline over the intervals tested." Finally, the statement concerning future research belongs in the discussion section.

Discussion

Whether the experiment was good or not is a judgment to be left to others. Also, an experiment can produce statistically significant differences and still be bad. No comparison was made in the experiment between dental appointments and consonant trigrams, and it is dangerous to make such comparisons between studies. Furthermore, the source of the consonant trigram data is not referenced.

Even if it were true that dental appointments were forgotten faster, this fact would only be *consistent* with an explanation based on repression; it would not necessarily *indicate* repression. Also, the linkage between repression and dental appointments would have to be explained. The reference to Freud needs a date. Finally, the last sentence is wrong, because the experiment could only support—not prove—such hypotheses, and because there was no demonstration either that the dental appointments were threatening or that memory for the dental appointments was affected. And the manuscript page header and page number are missing.

Table

The table heading is wrong—it should read "as a function of retention interval," not trials.

References

The format of the referenced article is wrong. APA style dictates the following format:

Peterson, L. R., & Peterson, M. J. (1959). Short-term retention of individual verbal items. Journal of Experimental Psychology, 58, 193–198.

In addition, the reference to Freud (cited in the discussion section) is missing.

CHAPTER 14

USING MULTIVARIATE DESIGN AND ANALYSIS

KEY QUESTIONS TO CONSIDER

- What statistics are used to evaluate correlational and experimental multivariate relationships?
- What are the key assumptions and requirements of multivariate statistics?
- How do various violations of the assumptions underlying multivariate statistics affect your data analysis?
- When is factor analysis used?
- Why are factors rotated in factor analysis?
- What do partial and part correlations tell you?
- For what research applications would you use the various types of multiple regression?
- How are multiple R and the regression weights used to interpret the results from a multiple regression analysis?
- How is the squared semipartial correlation used to interpret the results from a regression analysis?
- When would you use a multivariate analysis of variance to analyze your data?
- How are the results from a multivariate analysis of variance interpreted?
- When is loglinear analysis used to analyze your data?
- What is path analysis and how is it used in the research process?

CHAPTER OUTLINE

Experimental and Correlational Multivariate Designs
    Correlational Multivariate Design
    Experimental Multivariate Design
        Multivariate Statistical Tests
        Advantages of the Experimental Multivariate Strategy
        Advantages of the Correlational Multivariate Strategy
    Causal Inference
Assumptions and Requirements of Multivariate Statistics

REVIEW AND STUDY QUESTIONS

Key Term Definition

Define each of the following terms.

Univariate strategy:

Multivariate strategy:

Multiple regression:

Discriminant analysis:

Canonical correlation:

Factor analysis:

Multivariate analysis of variance (MANOVA):

Partial correlation:

Part correlation:

Multiple R:

R-square:

Beta weight:

Loglinear analysis:

Path analysis:

Multiple-Choice Questions

Circle the alternative that best completes the stem of each question.

1. An advantage of using multivariate analysis over separate univariate analyses is that using the multivariate analysis
   a. allows you to look at more complex relationships than does the univariate strategy.
   b. provides a more powerful test of your hypotheses.
   c. allows you not to worry about meeting restrictive assumptions characteristic of univariate statistics.
   d. both a and b

2. Path analysis is
   a. a unique statistical test that allows you to consider more than one dependent variable in an analysis.
   b. an application of multiple regression to the investigation of causal relationships among variables.
   c. not used to investigate causal relationships but is a multivariate statistic.
   d. an extension of the Pearson correlation to multivariate designs.

3. The presence of outliers in your data
   a. affects the magnitude of the correlations calculated but not the slope of the regression line.
   b. affects the slope of the regression line but not the magnitude of the correlations calculated.
   c. affects both the slope of the regression line and the magnitude of the correlations calculated.
   d. is less of a problem for multivariate statistics than it is for bivariate or univariate statistics.

4. An effective way of detecting outliers in a multivariate data set is to
   a. convert raw scores to z scores and evaluate the degree of deviance of the z scores.
   b. conduct individual Pearson correlations on your data before conducting any multivariate test.
   c. do nothing; outliers do not significantly affect multivariate statistics.
   d. both a and b

5. _____ occurs when variables in your analysis are highly correlated.
   a. Heteroscedasticity
   b. Multicollinearity
   c. Reflecting
   d. Outlier bias

6. _____ causes the observed value of a variable to differ to some extent from its true value.
   a. Homoscedasticity
   b. An outlier
   c. Error of measurement
   d. Multicollinearity

7. Generally speaking, multivariate analysis requires
   a. fairly large samples.
   b. small samples.
   c. less concern over meeting assumptions than do univariate tests.
   d. sampling from a population that is not normally distributed.

8. In a factor analysis the correlation between an individual variable and an underlying dimension is a
   a. discriminant function.
   b. factor loading.
   c. squared semipartial correlation.
   d. canonical function.

9. The factors extracted in a factor analysis are made more clear and interpretable by
   a. converting raw scores to z scores prior to analysis.
   b. eliminating variables that have low correlations with other variables.
   c. applying a square root transformation to the raw data prior to analysis.
   d. statistically rotating factors.

10. According to Tabachnick and Fidell (1989), principal components analysis could be used to
    a. help infer causality from correlational data.
    b. extract as many factors as possible from your data prior to a factor analysis.
    c. experiment with different communality values after an exploratory factor analysis.
    d. determine the degree of contribution of a variable in a multiple regression analysis.

11. _____ is a statistical technique used to evaluate the relationship between two variables statistically controlling the effects of a third.
    a. Discriminant analysis
    b. Canonical correlation
    c. Partial correlation
    d. Factor analysis

12. A statistical technique that involves entering multiple predictor variables into an equation according to a specified order determined by theory is
    a. hierarchical regression.
    b. simple regression.
    c. stepwise regression.
    d. none of the above

13. The use of stepwise regression techniques is frowned on because
    a. only three predictor variables can be entered at a time.
    b. it tends to be too sensitive to causal relationships among variables.
    c. it tends to capitalize on chance and may be limited to a particular sample.
    d. all of the above

14. If you have multiple predictor variables and a dichotomous dependent variable, the most appropriate multivariate test is
    a. stepwise regression.
    b. canonical correlation.
    c. factor analysis.
    d. discriminant analysis.

15. Loglinear analysis
    a. is a nonparametric statistic.
    b. works much like chi-square.
    c. can be used in place of ANOVA, MANOVA, or multiple regression where your data are categorical.
    d. all of the above

16. If you have two sets of variables to correlate, the most appropriate multivariate test is
    a. stepwise regression.
    b. canonical correlation.
    c. factor analysis.
    d. discriminant analysis.

17. Using a MANOVA in place of a univariate analysis for a within-subjects experiment is advantageous because MANOVA
    a. allows you to circumvent some of the restrictive assumptions of the univariate within-subjects ANOVA.
    b. allows you to include more than two independent variables in your analysis.
    c. uses separate error terms to test effects rather than a pooled error term.
    d. none of the above

18. In research situations in which you want to measure or manipulate categorical variables, an appropriate alternative to statistics such as ANOVA, MANOVA, or multiple regression would be
    a. canonical correlation.
    b. multiple t tests.
    c. path analysis.
    d. loglinear analysis.

Fill-In Questions

Fill in the blanks with the word or phrase that best completes each sentence.

1. If outliers in your data cause a negative skew, the most appropriate transformation strategy is to use a _____.

2. If an examination of a scatterplot of your data shows a conical pattern, then _____ _____ is present.

3. The most popular rotation strategy in factor analysis is _____.

4. _____ is a correlational technique that allows you to evaluate the relationship between two variables with the effects of a third removed from both of them.

5. The general linear equation formula is _____.

6. In the absence of any theoretical ordering of variables, _____ is the multiple regression strategy of choice.

7. _____ is the correlation between predicted values of Y and the observed values of Y, whereas _____ is the proportion of variability in the dependent variable that is accounted for by a set of predictors.

8. The _____ regression weights are usually used to interpret a significant regression analysis because they express differently scaled variables in the same terms.

9. Although a regression weight is often used as an index of the degree of contribution of a predictor variable, a better index is the _____.

10. The number of possible discriminant functions in a discriminant analysis is limited to _____ or to _____, whichever is less.

11. To determine the relationship between two sets of variables, you would use _____ _____.

12. The _____ produced in an SPSS-X MANOVA output are similar to factor loadings and can be used to evaluate the degree of contribution of a variable.

13. A path model that has causal relationships that run in only one direction and have no causal loops is called a(n) _____ model.

14. _____ are used to estimate the degree of causal relationship between variables in a path model.

15. _____ are followed when decomposing a path model into direct and indirect effects.

16. A test, analogous to chi-square, that you can use in place of ANOVA when your data are categorical is _____.

Essay Questions

1. Outline the major assumptions of multivariate statistics, and show how violations of each might affect the outcome of a multivariate analysis.

2. Compare and contrast partial and part correlation. What does each do with a third variable?

3. Discuss why stepwise multiple regression is the least preferred regression method.

4. Compare and contrast using unstandardized and standardized regression weights to evaluate the degree of contribution of a predictor to accounting for variance in the dependent variable. Is there a better alternative? Explain.

5. Briefly discuss the strategies that you could use to help interpret a significant main effect found with a MANOVA.

6. Describe several applications for loglinear analysis.

7. Draw diagrams of the various causal relationships discussed in the path analysis section of the text.

EXERCISING YOUR KNOWLEDGE

Which Multivariate Statistic Applies?

Here are several research examples. See if you can determine the best multivariate statistical test to apply. This task will be easier if you first identify the dependent variable(s), independent variables (if included), and predictor variables.

1. McKinney, Sprecher, and DeLamater (1984) were interested in the relationship between self-image and contraceptive behavior. A total of 985 college students was interviewed by telephone. Participants were asked questions that elicited information on body image, religiosity, age, number of intercourse partners, number of pregnancies, descriptions of the self, and the percent of lifetime intercourse experiences in which contraception was used.

2. To test the reactions of White males to interracial couples, Scott (1987) had either a same-race couple (White male–White female or Black male–Black female) or interracial couple (White male–Black female or Black male–White female) approach a White male participant. The couple approached the participant and asked for directions to a motel. As soon as the male of the couple finished speaking, he started a stopwatch unobtrusively. The latency to onset of the participant's directions and the duration of the directions given were recorded.

3. Post and Crowther (1985) were interested in the variables that could differentiate bulimic from nonbulimic girls. (Bulimia is an eating disorder characterized by repeated episodes of binge eating.) Post and Crowther administered several measures (Life History Questionnaire, Eating Attitudes Test, Self-Esteem Scale, Body Cathexis Scale, and the Beck Depression Inventory) to participants who were known to be either bulimic or nonbulimic. The central question of the research was which variables separated bulimics from nonbulimics.

4. In the first phase of a study of attitudes toward a nuclear power plant, Hughey, Sundstrom, and Lounsbury (1985) had participants rate the perceived likelihood of outcomes associated with a nuclear power plant (for example, traffic congestion, cheaper electricity, and so on). Each of 27 outcomes was rated for likelihood of occurrence on a seven-point scale. The main goal of the first part of this study was to determine which of the 27 rated outcomes were characteristic of underlying attitudes about the plant.

Sources

Hughey, J. B., Sundstrom, E., & Lounsbury, J. W. (1985). Attitudes toward nuclear power: A longitudinal analysis of expectancy-value models. *Basic and Applied Social Psychology, 6,* 75–91.

McKinney, K., Sprecher, S., & DeLamater, J. (1984). Self images and contraceptive behavior. *Basic and Applied Social Psychology, 5,* 37–57.

Post, G., & Crowther, J. H. (1985). Variables that discriminate bulimic from nonbulimic adolescent females. *Journal of Youth and Adolescence, 14,* 85–94.

Scott, R. R. (1987). Interracial couples: Situational factors in white males' reactions. *Basic and Applied Social Psychology, 8,* 125–138.

ANSWERS TO QUESTIONS AND EXERCISES

Multiple-Choice Questions

1.	D	9.	D	17.	A
2.	B	10.	B	18.	D
3.	C	11.	C		
4.	A	12.	A		
5.	B	13.	C		
6.	C	14.	D		
7.	A	15.	D		
8.	B	16.	B		

Fill-In Questions

1. reflecting strategy
2. heteroscedasticity
3. orthogonal rotation or varimax rotation
4. Partial correlation

5. $Y' = B_1 X_1 + B_2 X_2 + \cdots + \text{constant}$
6. simple regression
7. Multiple R; R-squared
8. standardized or beta
9. squared semipartial correlation
10. number of predictors; number of levels of the dependent variable minus 1
11. canonical correlation
12. structure correlations
13. recursive
14. Path coefficients
15. Wright's rules
16. loglinear analysis

Exercising Your Knowledge

1. The dependent (criterion variable) in this example is the percentage of intercourse experiences using contraception. The remaining variables are predictor variables. The most appropriate statistic is a simple multiple regression analysis because the dependent variable is continuous.

2. The design of this experiment was a one-factor, between-subjects with two dependent variables (latency and duration). Because of the multiple dependent variables, the most appropriate test here is a MANOVA.

3. There were several predictor variables in this study (for example, the Eating Attitudes Test, Life History Questionnaire) and a single dichotomous dependent variable (bulimic or nonbulimic participants). Consequently, the most appropriate multivariate statistical test is a discriminant analysis.

4. The aim of the first part of this study was to reduce a large number of measures to a smaller set by determining which outcomes constituted different attitudinal dimensions. To accomplish this task, the most appropriate statistic is a principal components analysis.

CHAPTER 15

USING THEORY

KEY QUESTIONS TO CONSIDER

- What is a theory?
- How does a theory differ from a hypothesis, a model, and a law?
- What is a computer model and what are the advantages of constructing one?
- How do mechanistic and functional explanations differ? Which type of explanation is better, and why?
- How do quantitative, qualitative, analogical, and fundamental theories differ?
- What are the various roles that theories play in science?
- How do you know a good theory from a bad one?
- What are the major steps involved in developing a theory, and what do you do at each step?
- What is meant by confirmation and disconfirmation of theories?
- How are theories effectively tested?
- What are the relative advantages and disadvantages of theory-driven and data-driven theories?

CHAPTER OUTLINE

What Is a Theory?
    Theory Versus Hypothesis
    Theory Versus Law
    Theory Versus Model
    Computer Modeling
    Mechanistic Versus Functional Explanations
Types of Theory
    Quantitative Versus Qualitative Theory
        Quantitative Theory
        Qualitative Theory
    Level of Description

REVIEW AND STUDY QUESTIONS

Key Term Definition

Define each of the following terms.

Theory:

Scientific theory:

Law:

Model:

Mechanistic explanation:

Functional explanation:

Quantitative theory:

Qualitative theory:

Descriptive theory:

Analogical theory:

Fundamental theory:

Domain:

Strong inference:

Confirmational strategy:

Disconfirmational strategy:

Multiple-Choice Questions

Circle the alternative that best completes the stem of each question.

1. A partially verified statement of a scientific relationship that cannot be directly observed is termed a
   a. hypothesis.
   b. theory.
   c. law.
   d. whatchamacallit.

170

2. The relationship described by a theory must be
   a. directly observed.
   b. deduced from a law.
   c. inferred from data.
   d. revealed by divine inspiration.

3. Theories are usually more _____ than hypotheses.
   a. complex
   b. simplified
   c. testable
   d. lawful

4. Most scientific laws represent
   a. theories that have been substantially verified.
   b. idealized empirically derived quantitative relationships.
   c. restrictions on behavior imposed by a governing body.
   d. partially verified relationships that cannot be directly observed.

5. A specific implementation of a more general theoretical view is referred to as a
   a. hypothesis.
   b. fact.
   c. law.
   d. model.

6. A _____ explanation describes an attribute or characteristic in terms of what it does for the organism.
   a. mechanistic
   b. functional
   c. operational
   d. reductionistic

7. A theory that specifies the variables and constants with which it works numerically is termed
   a. quantitative.
   b. qualitative.
   c. analogical.
   d. fundamental.

8. A theory that explained "drive" as a kind of pressure that built up in the organism like steam in a steam engine would be termed
   a. quantitative.
   b. qualitative.
   c. analogical.
   d. fundamental.

9. Theories differ in
   a. whether they are quantitative or qualitative.
   b. level of description.
   c. domain or scope.
   d. all of the above

10. Theory A attempts to describe how perceptual mechanisms of the visual system give rise to visual perceptions, including normal and illusory ones. Theory B attempts to account for the Mueller–Lyer illusion. We can say that, of the two theories, Theory A
    a. is more quantitative.
    b. is more qualitative.
    c. is more fundamental.
    d. has greater scope.

11. The role of theory in science is to
    a. provide understanding.
    b. provide a basis for prediction.
    c. guide research.
    d. all of the above

12. Although a wrong theory may fail to provide a true understanding of the phenomena with which it deals, it may nevertheless
    a. make correct predictions.
    b. provide a correct description of the underlying processes.
    c. give correct interpretations of the data.
    d. all of the above

13. If a theory provides ideas for new research, it is said to have
    a. moxie.
    b. schmaltz.
    c. heuristic value.
    d. serendipity.

14. A danger of letting theory guide the direction of research is that
    a. the data generated may have interest only in the context of the theory and therefore will become irrelevant if the theory is abandoned.
    b. theory is never a proper guide for research.
    c. the data generated by the research may not support the theory.
    d. theory cannot guide research.

15. A good theory should
    a. account for the existing data within its scope.
    b. offer good grounds for believing that predicted phenomena would occur under the specified conditions.
    c. be capable of failing some empirical test.
    d. all of the above

16. Theory A and Theory B account for the same range of phenomena and have the same degree of precision. However, Theory A requires five assumptions and Theory B only three. We can say that, relative to Theory A, Theory B is
    a. more heuristic.
    b. less heuristic.
    c. more parsimonious.
    d. less parsimonious.

17. In the course of theory construction, the hopeful theorist may use which of the following processes?
    a. preparation
    b. analogy
    c. introspection
    d. all of the above

18. A potential problem with using introspection to develop theories is that
    a. the act of trying to observe one's own mental processes may interfere with and distort those processes.
    b. observable mental events may play no causal role in the operation of the system being examined.
    c. important aspects of the system you are trying to observe may not produce observable mental activity.
    d. all of the above

19. If theory and data disagree,
    a. then the theory must be discarded.
    b. then the data must be discarded.
    c. then something is wrong.
    d. then both the theory and the data are wrong.

20. A theory
    a. is always right.
    b. can never be proven wrong.
    c. can never be proven right.
    d. is the same as a fact.

21. If a theory provides organization to the literature and has heuristic value, and there is nothing better to replace it, then
    a. even so, it will be scrapped if there is some evidence against it.
    b. it may continue to be promoted until a better theory is found, even though it is known to be wrong.
    c. it is probably correct.
    d. it is definitely incorrect.

Fill-In Questions

Fill in the blanks with the word or phrase that best completes each sentence.

1. A(n) _____ is a partially verified statement of a scientific relationship that cannot be directly observed.

2. A specific implementation of a more general theoretical view is termed a(n) _____ _____.

3. An application of a general theory to a specific situation is termed a(n) _____ _____.

4. A good way to determine what behavior a theory predicts under given circumstances is to construct a _____.

5. Any theory that is not quantitative is _____.

6. A(n) _____ theory merely describes relationships.

7. A(n) _____ theory explains a relationship by borrowing from well-understood models.

8. The range of situations to which a theory may be legitimately applied is its _____ _____.

9. A theory that is capable of failing an empirical test is said to be _____.

10. A theory is _____ if it accounts for a phenomenon with few assumptions.

11. _____ refers to the degree to which you are prepared by experience to recognize the solution to a theoretical problem.

12. When you interpret animal behavior in terms of the motivations and emotions of people, you are _____.

13. When you test a theory by looking for evidence that supports it, you are using a(n) _____ strategy.

14. When you test a theory by looking for evidence that contradicts it, you are using a(n) _____ strategy.

15. Platt (1964) referred to a process of proposing alternative theories, eliminating one or more of them through experimental tests and continuing until one theory remained. He termed this process _____.

16. Research that is organized around testing the specific implications of a theory is said to be _____ driven.

Essay Questions

1. Give five advantages of a computer model.

2. Describe how to develop an analogical theory.

3. List the characteristics of a good theory.

4. Give the five steps involved in developing a theory.

5. Contrast the confirmational and disconfirmational strategies of theory testing. Give an example of each.

EXERCISING YOUR KNOWLEDGE

The Confirmation Bias

When testing theories or hypotheses, we tend to search for evidence that confirms rather than disconfirms. You can see this "confirmation bias" in operation by conducting the following brief demonstration (suggested by Bolt & Myers, 1987, based on an experiment reported by Wason, 1981) on your hapless friends and relatives.

All you need is four index cards, marked as follows:

Card	Front	Back
1	D	3
2	3	D
3	B	6
4	7	D

Arrange the cards on a table with the front sides up and show them to your victim. Then give the following instructions:

Each card has a letter on one side and a number on the other. There is a rule relating the two. The rule might be this: If there is a D on one side of a card, then there is a 3 on the other side. You can test this rule by turning the cards over one at a time, but you can turn over only two of the cards. Choose two cards and turn them over. From the evidence, decide whether the rule is correct or incorrect. You should note which card is turned over first and second, and what decision was reached.

Try the demonstration with several people.

Sources

Bolt, M., & Myers, D. G. (1987). *Instructor's Manual to Accompany Myers: Social Psychology (second edition).* New York: McGraw-Hill.

Wason, P. C. (1981). The importance of cognitive illusions. *Quarterly Journal of Experimental Psychology, 4,* 356.

Types of Theories

Go to the library and find an example of each of the different types of theories discussed in Chapter 15 (for example, descriptive, quantitative, and so on). What about the theory causes it to fall into a particular category? Could you suggest modifications to the theory to change its classification (for example, from a qualitative to a quantitative theory)?

ANSWERS TO QUESTIONS AND EXERCISES

Multiple-Choice Questions

1. B	7. A	12. A	17. D
2. C	8. C	13. C	18. D
3. A	9. D	14. A	19. C
4. B	10. D	15. D	20. C
5. D	11. D	16. C	21. B
6. B			

Fill-In Questions

1. theory
2. model
3. model
4. computer model
5. qualitative
6. descriptive
7. analogical
8. domain or scope
9. testable
10. parsimonious
11. Preparedness

12. anthropomorphizing
13. confirmational
14. disconfirmational
15. strong inference
16. theory

Exercising Your Knowledge

The Confirmation Bias

Most people will begin by turning over the first card (with the D showing) in order to confirm that there is a 3 on the other side, as stated by the rule. The second card selected is usually the one showing the 3. Turning this card over reveals a D. Most people find this evidence quite conclusive as it again confirms that a 3 and D occur together. However, this evidence actually adds nothing beyond what was learned in the first test. Had the letter on the back side been, for example, a B, it would not have disproved the rule. Perhaps every D has a 3, but some Bs have 3s too!

The proper card to select is card 4, with the 7 showing. If there is a D on the bottom side, then the rule is incorrect. Choosing card 4 is a disconfirmation strategy: If the rule is correct, then there will *not* be a D. If your participant chose card 4, give him or her a pat on the back. Most of us have a strong bias to look for confirmatory rather than disconfirmatory evidence, yet it is disconfirmation that provides the most powerful test of a theory.

CHAPTER 16

MAKING SENSE OF RESEARCH

KEY QUESTIONS TO CONSIDER

- What are the criteria for acceptance of a manuscript?
- How does peer review work, and what are some of the problems associated with it?
- How do you play the "publication game"?
- What are research fads and why do they emerge and die?
- What makes certain research areas more popular than others?
- What constitutes fraud in research and how prevalent is it?
- Why do scientists sometimes engage in fraudulent research practices?
- What steps can be taken to reduce the problem of fraud in research?
- How do values enter into the scientific process?
- How can scientists guard against values entering into their research?
- What is meta-analysis and how does it differ from a traditional literature review?
- What are the steps involved in conducting a meta-analysis?
- What are some of the problems associated with meta-analysis, and how can they be dealt with?

CHAPTER OUTLINE

Publication Practices
    Criteria for Acceptance of a Manuscript
        Statistical Significance
        Consistency With Previous Knowledge
        Significance of the Contribution
        Editorial Policy
    Pernicious Problems of Peer Review
        Peer Review
        Problems With Peer Review
    Playing the Publication Game

REVIEW AND STUDY QUESTIONS

Key Term Definition

Define each of the following terms.

File drawer phenomenon:

Paradigm:

Normal science:

Paradigm shift:

Peer review:

Research fad:

Research trend:

Traditional literature review:

Meta-analysis:

Multiple-Choice Questions

Circle the alternative that best completes the stem of each question.

1. For a research article to be deemed acceptable for publication in a journal,
   a. the paper must offer new information, not merely replicate old findings.
   b. the findings must be reliable as shown by replication or statistical significance.
   c. the findings must derive from acceptable methodology.
   d. all of the above

2. The file drawer phenomenon results when
   a. unpublished research is later published because new findings render the results important.
   b. studies having statistically nonsignificant results are not submitted for publication.
   c. studies accumulate in the file drawer because the investigator lacks the time to write them up and submit them for publication.
   d. important findings get lost in the file drawer, to be discovered only after someone else has replicated the findings.

3. When an independent variable actually has *no* effect on a dependent variable, the results are difficult to publish because
   a. it is not important to know which variables are ineffective in a given paradigm.
   b. such results must be shown to be significantly nonsignificant at the 0.05 level.
   c. you must demonstrate that the failure to show an effect is not due to poor methodology.
   d. all of the above

4. Anomalous findings (those that do not appear to make sense within the currently accepted framework)
   a. are usually accepted immediately by the research community.
   b. usually call into question the research that produced them.
   c. immediately overturn the currently accepted framework.
   d. by their very nature are never reliable.

5. According to Kuhn (1964), normal science consists of
   a. extending the organized body of knowledge along the lines delineated by the current paradigm.
   b. shifting from one paradigm to another as each new fact dooms the previous paradigm to oblivion.
   c. finding radical new interpretations of existing data.
   d. making a significant new discovery each day by 5 P.M.

6. To be accepted for publication, a research paper today usually must contain
   a. no more than a single experiment involving a treatment and a control condition.
   b. a series of experiments or at least a parametric study involving several levels of two or more variables.
   c. citations praising the research conducted by the editor and the reviewers.
   d. a significant new theoretical formulation.

7. The practice of insisting on multiple experiments in a research paper
   a. increases the paper's contribution to knowledge.
   b. increases the chances that reviewers will find fault with the paper.
   c. delays getting important findings out.
   d. all of the above

8. To ensure that reviewers of research papers can make their judgments without fear of reprisal, reviews are often
   a. biased in favor of the author of the paper.
   b. conducted by a computer.
   c. conducted anonymously.
   d. kept under lock and key.

9. Mahoney (1977) reported that a paper was consistently rated higher if its results
   a. were interpreted by the author as supporting the reviewer's theoretical view.
   b. supported the reviewer's theoretical view.
   c. contradicted current theoretical views.
   d. contradicted the reviewer's private beliefs.

10. Empirical studies have consistently found that the correlation between reviewer judgments concerning the acceptability of a manuscript for publication is
   a. extremely high, showing good reliability.
   b. moderately high, showing reasonable reliability.
   c. low, showing poor reliability.
   d. negative, showing that reviewers always disagree.

11. When Peters and Ceci (1982) submitted twelve previously published articles to the journals in which the articles were originally published, they found that
   a. all but one of the resubmissions were recognized.
   b. only three of the resubmissions were recognized and rejected for this reason.
   c. eight of the undetected papers were rejected for publication, usually on the grounds that they were methodologically flawed.
   d. both b and c

12. To get your research study published, you should
   a. do good research.
   b. tackle important questions.
   c. write clearly.
   d. do all of the above

13. If reviews of your research article are unfavorable and you feel that your paper has been unfairly criticized, you should
   a. sue the journal for damages.
   b. complain to the president of the American Psychological Association.
   c. write to the editor asking him or her to reconsider, and document the deficiencies in the reviews.
   d. give up research and become a stockbroker.

14. Fads in research often emerge when
   a. a new phenomenon is discovered or a new way to study a previously difficult topic is identified.
   b. progress in an area becomes more difficult because the "easy gold" has been found.
   c. researchers settle down to the "pick and shovel" work of normal science.
   d. researchers agree which findings are reliable and which interpretations are sound.

15. A research area usually decreases in popularity when
    a. it is felt that important aspects of the problem have been solved.
    b. the research appears to lead to an empirical dead end.
    c. research in the area is shown to be flawed by artifacts and poor methodology.
    d. all of the above

16. To be most effective in the long run as a scientist, you should
    a. become a slave to fads.
    b. jump from one research area to another so as to follow the trends and grant money.
    c. identify an important research area and stick with it.
    d. become a journal editor.

17. According to the text, fraud in research comprises
    a. outright fabrication of data.
    b. altering data to make them look better.
    c. publishing stolen work.
    d. all of the above
    e. both a and b only

18. According to Bell (1992) a major factor contributing to fraud in research is
    a. competition for scarce research funding.
    b. that most scientists are dishonest.
    c. the need for scientists to boost their egos.
    d. all of the above

19. According to the text, the best way to guard against fraud in research is to
    a. make the penalties for fraud more severe.
    b. stress that ethical research practice involves honesty during training of scientists.
    c. use the peer review process to detect fraud.
    d. none of the above

20. If one's culture or personal beliefs affect the decision concerning how to study behavior, we say that
    a. research fraud has occurred.
    b. the resulting research is objective.
    c. values have affected science.
    d. none of the above

21. Longino (1990) suggests that which of the following is a factor influencing the course of science?
    a. Values affect which questions are addressed and which are ignored.
    b. Value-laden terms affect how data are described.
    c. Values affect the basic assumptions that scientists make about the phenomena they study.
    d. all of the above
    e. both a and b only

22. To conduct a meta-analysis, you must first
    a. locate the relevant research to review.
    b. identify relevant variables.
    c. conduct the meta-analysis proper.
    d. sharpen your pencil.

23. To discover the extent to which the file drawer phenomenon may bias your meta-analysis, you should
    a. identify the researchers in the area under investigation and ask them if they have any unpublished research of relevance to the topic.
    b. estimate the extent of the impact of the file drawer phenomenon on your analysis.
    c. ask journal editors for a list of all manuscripts on the topic that have been rejected because of a lack of statistical significance.
    d. either a or b

24. Cooper and Rosenthal (1980) found that participants using a meta-analysis (in contrast to those using a traditional analysis) were
    a. more likely to conclude that the independent variable under examination was effective.
    b. less likely to conclude that the independent variable under examination was effective.
    c. positive that the independent variable was effective.
    d. less likely to reject the null hypothesis.

Fill-In Questions

Fill in the blanks with the word or phrase that best completes each sentence.

1. Because of the file drawer phenomenon, published findings as a group may be _____ _____ reliable than they seem.

2. Before accepting a negative finding, editors and reviewers want proof that the failure to obtain a statistically significant effect was not due to _____.

3. Results of a study are less likely to be accepted for publication if they fail to show _____ _____ with previous knowledge.

4. Kuhn (1964) termed the overthrow of an old view by a new one a(n) _____ _____.

5. When determining whether to accept or reject a paper, editors and reviewers must assess the degree to which the reported findings contribute to the _____ of _____.

6. _____ is the practice of having other researchers in the area judge whether or not a research paper should be published.

7. A(n) _____ is a sustained research effort that gradually changes the focus of research in an area as knowledge accumulates.

8. List two factors that influence research fraud: _____ and _____.

9. According to the text, values can creep into science when scientists move from _____ to _____.

10. A set of statistical procedures that allow you to combine or compare the results from different studies is termed a(n) _____.

Essay Questions

1. List the four criteria for acceptance of a manuscript that were given in the text.

2. Discuss the problems that arise from peer review of research manuscripts. How do these problems affect the published literature?

3. Indicate the steps you can take to increase the chances your research paper will be accepted for publication.

4. Give five reasons why a research area decreases in popularity.

5. Discuss the problem of fraud in research. What constitutes fraud, how prevalent is it, and how can it be reduced?

6. Define meta-analysis, and outline the steps you should follow when conducting one.

EXERCISING YOUR KNOWLEDGE

Fads and Trends in Research

Chapter 16 discusses the issue of how some research areas wax and wane in popularity. For this exercise find a research area (either one that is popular today or one that was popular in the past) and trace its course in the research literature. This can be done by performing a content analysis on the listings in the *Psychological Abstracts* (similar to the one done on cognitive dissonance theory reported in the text). Some ideas on possible research are

1. The research controversy studied by both Hull and Tolman in the 1940s on the nature of learning

2. The research conducted during the 1960s and 1970s on teaching language to nonhuman primates

3. The research on eyewitness identification

4. The research conducted during the 1960s and 1970s on helping in emergencies

For whatever topic you choose consider the following:

1. Has the amount of research done in the area decreased, increased, or stayed the same?

2. What factors do you think account for the change (or stability) in the research area?

3. Would you define the line of research investigated a "trend" or a "fad"? Justify your categorization by discussing why the research is either a fad or a trend.

ANSWERS TO QUESTIONS AND EXERCISES

Multiple-Choice Questions

1.	D	13.	C
2.	B	14.	A
3.	C	15.	D
4.	B	16.	C
5.	A	17.	D
6.	B	18.	A
7.	D	19.	B
8.	C	20.	C
9.	B	21.	D
10.	C	22.	B
11.	D	23.	D
12.	D	24.	A

Fill-In Questions

1. less
2. improper procedures
3. consistency
4. paradigm shift
5. advancement; knowledge
6. Peer review
7. research trend
8. competition for funding, tenure pressures, elitism
9. what is; what ought to be
10. meta-analysis

APPENDIX
FEEDBACK TABLES FOR
HYPOTHESIS-TESTING EXERCISE

TABLE 1   FEEDBACK MATRIX FOR HYPOTHESIS 1

Column

	1	2	3	4	5	6	7	8	9	
1	Y	N	N	Y	N	N	Y	N	N	1
2	N	N	N	N	N	N	N	N	N	2
3	N	N	N	N	N	N	N	N	N	3
4	Y	N	N	Y	N	N	Y	N	N	4
5	N	N	N	N	N	N	N	N	N	5
6	N	N	N	N	N	N	N	N	N	6
7	Y	N	N	Y	N	N	Y	N	N	7
8	N	N	N	N	N	N	N	N	N	8
9	N	N	N	N	N	N	N	N	N	9
	1	2	3	4	5	6	7	8	9	

Row

TABLE 2   FEEDBACK MATRIX FOR HYPOTHESIS 2

Column

	1	2	3	4	5	6	7	8	9	
1	N	N	N	N	N	N	N	N	N	1
2	N	N	N	N	N	N	N	N	N	2
3	N	N	N	N	N	N	N	N	N	3
4	N	N	N	N	N	N	N	N	N	4
5	N	N	N	Y	Y	Y	N	N	N	5
6	N	N	N	N	N	N	N	N	N	6
7	N	N	N	N	N	N	N	N	N	7
8	N	N	N	Y	Y	Y	N	N	N	8
9	N	N	N	N	N	N	N	N	N	9
	1	2	3	4	5	6	7	8	9	

Row

TABLE 3   FEEDBACK MATRIX FOR HYPOTHESIS 3

Column

	1	2	3	4	5	6	7	8	9	
1	Y	Y	Y	Y	Y	Y	Y	Y	Y	1
2	N	N	N	N	N	N	N	N	N	2
3	N	N	N	N	N	N	N	N	N	3
4	N	N	N	N	N	N	N	N	N	4
5	Y	Y	Y	Y	Y	Y	Y	Y	Y	5
6	N	N	N	N	N	N	N	N	N	6
7	N	N	N	N	N	N	N	N	N	7
8	N	N	N	N	N	N	N	N	N	8
9	Y	Y	Y	Y	Y	Y	Y	Y	Y	9
	1	2	3	4	5	6	7	8	9	

Row

SOLUTIONS TO HYPOTHESIS DEVELOPMENT PROBLEMS

Problem 1:   Single cross

Problem 2:   Two black figures

Problem 3:   As many figures as borders